BRIDGING THE HIGHER EDUCATION DIVIDE

BRIDGING THE HIGHER EDUCATION DIVIDE

Strengthening Community Colleges and Restoring the American Dream

The Report of The Century Foundation Task Force on Preventing Community Colleges from Becoming Separate and Unequal

With background papers by Sandy Baum and Charles Kurose; Sara Goldrick-Rab and Peter Kinsley; Tatiana Melguizo and Holly Kosiewicz

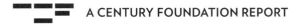 A CENTURY FOUNDATION REPORT

NEW YORK | THE CENTURY FOUNDATION PRESS

LIBRARY OF CONGRESS CATALOGING-IN-PUBLICATION DATA
Available from the publisher upon request.

Manufactured in the United States of America

Cover and text design by Abigail Grimshaw

Foreword

In our nation's struggle to promote social mobility and widen the circle of people who can enjoy the American Dream, education has always been a key driver; and no set of educational institutions embodies the promise of equal opportunity more than our country's community colleges. Two-year colleges have opened the doors of higher education for low-income and working-class students as never before, and yet, as the pages that follow make clear, community colleges often fail to provide the conditions for student success.

There are many important efforts underway to improve the outcomes of students in community colleges, largely focused on initiatives to scale up promising reforms. But there has also been a gaping hole in the dialogue: few people have been analyzing the growing racial and economic stratification between two- and four-year colleges, and the harmful consequences of those divisions.

The Century Foundation Task Force on Preventing Community Colleges from Becoming Separate and Unequal faces those grave realities in unblinking fashion. The Task Force is very fortunate to have benefited from the extraordinary leadership of its co-chairs, Anthony Marx, the president of the New York Public Library and the former president of Amherst College, and Eduardo Padrón, the president of Miami Dade College. Padrón has been a brilliant and innovative leader of the nation's largest institution of higher education; and Marx has been the conscience of the four-year sector, helping to put the issue of socioeconomic diversity and community college transfers on the national agenda. As a team, they helped lead the Task Force to come to consensus around a series of bold and efficacious recommendations.

This Task Force is the latest in a long line of research supported by Century seeking ways to promote equal opportunity from the preschool level through postsecondary education. Our research on early education and K–12 schooling includes *A Notion at Risk: Preserving Public Education as an Engine for Social Mobility*, edited by Century senior fellow Richard D. Kahlenberg; *All Together Now: Creating Middle-Class Schools through Public School Choice*, by Kahlenberg; *Divided We Fail: Coming Together through Public School Choice*, the report of the Century Task Force on the Common School; *Public School Choice v. Private School Vouchers*, edited by Kahlenberg; *Improving on No Child Left Behind: Getting Education Reform Back on Track*, edited by Kahlenberg; *In Plain Sight: Simple, Difficult Lessons from New Jersey's Expensive Efforts to Close the Achievement Gap*, by Gordon MacInnes; *Spin Cycle: How Research Is Used in Policy Decisions: The Case of Charter Schools*, by Jeffrey R. Henig; *Diverse Charter Schools: Can Racial and Socioeconomic Integration Promote Better Outcomes for Students*, by Kahlenberg and Halley Potter; *The Future of School Integration: Socioeconomic Diversity as an Education Reform Strategy*, edited by Kahlenberg; and *Beyond the Education Wars: Evidence that Collaboration Builds Effective Schools*, by Greg Anrig.

At the higher education level, we have also produced an important set of books and reports, three volumes edited by Kahlenberg (*America's Untapped Resource: Low-Income Students in Higher Education*; *Rewarding Strivers: Helping Low-Income Students Succeed in College*; and *Affirmative Action for the Rich: Legacy Preferences in College Admissions*), as well as *A Better Affirmative Action: State Universities that Created Alternatives to Racial Preferences*, by Kahlenberg and Potter. Because much of our higher education work at Century has focused on increasing access to selective four-year institutions, we were eager to supplement that line of research with the present report on community colleges—institutions that educate increasingly large numbers of low-income, working class, immigrant, and minority students.

We are very grateful to the Ford Foundation, whose generous support made the work of this Task Force possible. In particular, we would like to extend warm thanks to Jeannie Oakes and Douglas Wood of Ford for their powerful insights and support of our work.

In addition, we are thankful for the advice and participation of three key officials in the U.S. Department of Education who, while not members of the Task Force, attended meetings of the group and shared valuable thoughts: Martha Kanter, Seth Galanter, and Michael Dannenberg.

The Task Force was fortunate to be supported by the superb research of three sets of authors: Sandy Baum of George Washington University and Charles Kurose, an independent consultant for the College Board; Sara Goldrick-Rab and Peter Kinsley of the University of Wisconsin at Madison; and Tatiana Melguizo and Holly Kosiewicz of the University of Southern California.

The entire enterprise was guided from start to finish by Century's Richard Kahlenberg, who served as executive director of the Task Force, with critical assistance from Halley Potter, policy associate at Century.

Most of all, I want to thank the twenty-two members of the Task Force, led by Anthony Marx and Eduardo Padrón. The group includes distinguished representatives from two-year and four-year colleges, scholars of higher education, and representatives of the business, philanthropic, and civil rights communities. Their hard work produced a bold set of recommendations, which, if followed, have the potential to restart the community college sector as an engine for social mobility.

—Janice Nittoli, President
The Century Foundation
April 2013

Contents

Members of the Task Force

Anthony W. Marx, Task Force Co-Chair
President, The New York Public Library; Former President, Amherst College

Eduardo J. Padrón, Task Force Co-Chair
President, Miami Dade College

John Brittain
Law Professor, University of the District of Columbia, David A. Clarke School of Law;
Former Chief Counsel, Lawyers' Committee for Civil Rights

Walter G. Bumphus
President and CEO, American Association of Community Colleges

Michele Cahill
Vice President, National Program, and Program; Director, Urban Education,
Carnegie Corporation of New York

Louis Caldera
Former President, University of New Mexico; Former Secretary of the Army

Patrick M. Callan
President, Higher Education Policy Institute

Nancy Cantor
Chancellor, Syracuse University

Samuel D. Cargile
Vice President, Senior Advisor to CEO, Lumina Foundation

Anthony P. Carnevale
Director, Georgetown University Center on Education and the Workforce

Michelle Asha Cooper
President, Institute for Higher Education Policy

Sara Goldrick-Rab
Associate Professor of Education Policy Studies and Sociology,
University of Wisconsin–Madison

Jerome Karabel
Professor of Sociology, University of California–Berkeley

Catherine Koshland
Vice Provost of Teaching, Learning, Academic Planning and Facilities,
University of California– Berkeley

Félix V. Matos Rodríguez
President, Eugenio María de Hostos Community College of
The City University of New York

Gail Mellow
President, LaGuardia Community College of The City University of New York

Arthur J. Rothkopf
President Emeritus, Lafayette College; Former Senior Vice President,
U.S. Chamber of Commerce

Sandra Schroeder
President, AFT Washington; Professor, Seattle Central Community College

Louis Soares
Senior Fellow, Center for American Progress; Former Director of Business
Development, State of Rhode Island

Suzanne Walsh
Senior Program Officer, Postsecondary Success, Bill and Melinda Gates Foundation

Ronald Williams
Vice President, The College Board; Former President, Prince George's
Community College

Joshua Wyner
Executive Director, College Excellence Program, Aspen Institute

Richard D. Kahlenberg, *Executive Director*
Senior Fellow, The Century Foundation

Report of the Task Force

Executive Summary

THE COMMUNITY COLLEGE CHALLENGE

American community colleges stand at the confluence of four mighty rivers that are profoundly influencing all of American life. At a time of growing economic globalization, community colleges are a critical element in the strategy to address the skills and education gap to meet the emerging needs of industries in the new knowledge economy. At a time of stagnant social mobility, two-year open-access institutions are pivotal in efforts to restore the American Dream. At a time when rising college costs are making some four-year institutions seem beyond reach for many students, community colleges remain a relatively affordable option for millions of Americans. And, at a time of deep demographic change that is making obsolete the very term *minority*, community colleges educate nearly half of America's undergraduates of color.

In striving for the Obama administration's goal of raising postsecondary graduation rates to be first in the world by 2020—so that 60 percent of 25–34 year olds have a postsecondary credential—community colleges are expected to shoulder the bulk of the challenge. Of 8 million new degrees required to reach the goal, the Obama administration expects 5 million (or 63 percent) to come from the community college sector.

Yet, for reasons outlined below, public community colleges, which serve some 11 million students and 44 percent of the U.S. college population, often are not equipped for the challenge. Although many community colleges do a superb job of serving disadvantaged populations, on the whole, the college "dropout" rate for American students might be as high as 50 percent—far higher than the high school dropout rate—and community college dropout rates are higher still. While 81.4 percent of students entering community college for the first time say they eventually want to transfer and earn at least a bachelor's degree, only 11.6 percent of them do so within six years.

A central problem is that two-year colleges are asked to educate those students with the greatest needs, using the least funds, and in increasingly separate and unequal institutions. Our higher education system, like the larger society, is growing more and more unequal. We need radical innovations that redesign institutions and provide necessary funding tied to performance.

Lessons from Elementary and Secondary Education

In the K–12 realm, racial and economic stratification has long been recognized as a major impediment to equal opportunity, and policymakers have sought to address the issue by reducing separation (through racial and economic school integration programs) and by providing additional funding to schools with concentrations of poverty.

In the landmark *Brown v. Board of Education* decision in 1954, a unanimous U.S. Supreme Court famously recognized that separate schools for black and white children were inherently unequal. Today, social science research suggests that economic segregation in schools is highly detrimental: for any given student, attending a higher-poverty school predicts significantly lower outcomes.

In response, many school districts have created "magnet" schools to attract middle-class students into economically disadvantaged schools; and they allow low-income students to transfer to higher-performing middle-class schools. Both sets of strategies are associated with considerably higher achievement for low-income students and no decline in the achievement of middle-class students.

Likewise, federal policy, dating back to the 1965 Elementary and Secondary Education Act, has recognized that children in higher-poverty schools deserve extra resources, and hundreds of billions of dollars in Title I funds have been devoted to providing aid to higher-poverty schools. In part because of litigation on behalf of low-income students, state funding formulas in K–12 education routinely provide additional spending for low-income students. Nationally, more than two-thirds of all states provide additional funding for low-income students or students in need of remedial education, most commonly awarding 25 percent more.

Addressing Stratification in Higher Education

The distinction between K–12 and higher education policy on the issue of racial and economic stratification between institutions is striking. Elite higher education has recognized the need to integrate by race, adopting affirmative action programs to enhance the representation of African American and Latino students, but there has been no comparable effort to integrate by socioeconomic status. And there is little deliberate effort to draw more middle and upper-middle class students to community colleges, as "magnet schools" work to do at the K–12 level. Likewise, there is no comparable effort to provide extra federal and state resources to community colleges analogous to federal Title I funding or state-level adequacy funding at the K–12 level. To the contrary, state and federal resources tilt toward colleges with more advantaged student populations.

On one level, it is understandable that higher education has been slow to address issues of stratification. While primary and secondary schools have long educated a broad cross section of the American public, the entire higher education sector was fairly elite until recently. Today, however, as more and more students attend college, stratification issues loom much larger. Paradoxically, increasing college access is increasing inequality within the higher education universe. High-socioeconomic status (SES) students outnumber low-SES students by 14 to 1 in the most competitive four-year institutions, yet low-SES students outnumber high-SES students in community colleges by nearly 2 to 1.

The increasing economic and racial stratification of colleges and universities is troubling because largely separate educational systems for mostly rich and white students, and for mostly poor and minority students, are rarely equal. Racial and economic stratification is connected to unequal financial resources as well as to unequal curricula, expectations, and school cultures. Low-income and working-class people generally wield less power in our political system, and institutions serving them are often short-changed on resources. For example, between 1999 and 2009, per-pupil total operating expenditures increased by almost $14,000 for private research universities, while public community colleges saw just a $1 increase (in 2009 dollars).

With fewer financial resources, and often with a different curriculum and set of expectations, schools that are racially and economically isolated often produce poor results. For one thing, researchers have documented a reduction in the chances of ultimately earning a bachelor's degree associated with a given individual beginning at a community college as compared with a four-year institution, controlling for a student's level of preparation. Likewise, there is suggestive evidence from within the universe of two-year colleges that racial and socioeconomic isolation can negatively affect the performance of any given student. These poor outcomes are unacceptable given that community college is often the only realistic option of postsecondary education for low-income students.

The theoretical justification for our stratified system of higher education with differing levels of funding is that it allows different types of institutions to focus on what they do best. Four-year institutions will cater to the most highly prepared students, the theory suggests, and two-year institutions will educate large numbers of less-prepared students to their own levels of success focusing on technical degrees and certificates. This division of duties has some merit, but the evidence suggests that a system that lacks fluidity and underfunds community colleges is neither equitable nor efficient.

RECOMMENDATIONS FOR CHANGE

Although the challenges are considerable, we have great optimism that if critical innovations are made to the design and financing of community colleges, and if bold changes are undertaken to address the increasing economic and racial isolation of students, two-year colleges can build further their vital role as engines of social mobility and economic competitiveness for students from all backgrounds. In short, they can become America's quintessential "middle-class" institutions—serving both those already in the middle-class and those aspiring to become part of it.

It is time for innovative thinking, centered around redesigned institutions, greater transparency of funding, incentives for greater access, and more substantial investments tied to performance. Although most policymakers and institutional leaders focus on highlighting, sharing, and scaling best practices at successful community colleges—something we support—we need to go beyond that limited approach and offer bold and innovative thinking that is also efficacious.

In particular, our two central recommendations suggest ways (1) to create new outcomes-based funding in higher education, with a much greater emphasis on providing additional public supports based on student needs; and (2) to reduce the racial and economic stratification between two- and four-year institutions.

Innovations in Accountability and Funding

In order to make funding more equitable and to provide community colleges with the resources necessary to boost completion (and thereby raise overall efficiency), we recommend the following innovations.

Adopt State and Federal "Adequacy"-Based Funding in Higher Education Akin to That Used in Primary and Secondary Education, Combined with Considerations of Outcomes. We propose tying new accountability plans to greater funding in higher education for institutions serving those students with the greatest needs. In short, we need a K–12 Title I–type program for higher education, coupled with considerations of student outcomes, such as job placements, degrees earned, and transfers to four- year institutions. In order to promote equity and avoid incentives for "creaming" the most well prepared students, funding should be tied to distance traveled and progress made—that is to say, consideration of where students start as well as where they end up. In addition, the number of nontraditional, minority and low-income students who achieve each of these outcomes should be monitored. Accountability, coupled with adequate funding, should encourage a necessary redesign of the way in which community colleges deliver education.

Establish Greater Transparency Regarding Public Financial Subsidies to Higher Education. In order to bring greater clarity to all types of public support for higher education, we call on the U.S. Departments of Education and the Treasury to issue a report on the extent of public subsidies to various types of institutions—and the accompanying benefit to different socioeconomic populations—including public tax expenditures in the form of tax breaks for private donations, tax exemptions for endowment-derived income, and the like. The intent of this transparency is not to reduce funding for four-year institutions but to detail more vividly the ways in which many community colleges deserve greater public support.

Innovations in Governance to Reduce Economic and Racial Stratification in Higher Education and Strengthen the Connections between Two- and Four-Year Institutions

Our second set of recommendations goes beyond the issue of unequal financing to address underlying the issue of economic and racial stratification itself. Economic and racial hierarchies—in which wealthy and white students trend toward selective four-year colleges and working-class and minority students trend toward community colleges—are familiar, but they are in no sense natural or inevitable. We recommend the following reforms.

Encourage the Growth of Redesigned Institutions That Facilitate the Connection between Community Colleges and Four-Year Colleges. Among the most promising strategies of reducing stratification is to find ways to connect what are now separate two- and four-year institutional silos. Strengthening the ties between institutions could have the effect not only of reducing the economic and racial stratification of the student populations, but also would, by definition, reduce institutional stratification itself. By strengthening connections between two- and four-year institutions, fewer students would be lost in what can often be a difficult process of moving to four-year settings, in which credits fail to transfer with students and different financial aid policies may exist. By blending elements of two- and four-year colleges in one setting—such as by creating bachelor's degree programs that are delivered jointly by two- and four-year institutions and require only a single point of entry in the freshman year—institutions may also draw a broader cross section of students than community colleges do.

Take Concrete Steps to Facilitate Community College Transfer. To facilitate movement from two- to four-year institutions, we believe states should promote "guaranteed transfer" policies; states and/or the federal government should offer financial incentives to four-year colleges that accept economically disadvantaged community college transfer students; four-year institutions should provide a clear, predictable pathway for students to transfer from community colleges; and highly selective four-year colleges and universities should commit to accepting community college transfers for 5 percent of their junior class.

Encourage Innovation in Racially and Economically Inclusive Community College Honors Programs. Honors programs are an important "magnet" feature of community colleges, a way of reducing both racial and economic stratification. If one objective of having an honors program is to draw talented students from a range of economic and racial backgrounds, the challenge is to offer programs that simultaneously will be highly attractive to students who might not otherwise consider community college and yet at the same time avoid becoming tracking devices that segregate students within community colleges.

Encourage Innovation in Early College Programs that Enhance Community College Diversity. "Early college" programs, some of which allow talented high school students to take advanced courses at community colleges, may provide a way of attracting high-achieving and middle-class populations to community colleges that are racially and economically isolated. We recommend federal funding of those early college programs that would have the effect of better integrating two-year institutions that are racially and economically isolated.

Prioritize Funding of New Programs for Economically and Racially Isolated Community Colleges. In addition to addressing stratification between the community college and four-year college sectors, there is the additional issue of socioeconomic and racial stratification between individual two-year institutions. Because many low-income community college students have little choice in where they will attend college, we recommend that state and federal funding programs for honors programs, early college, and other initiatives be directed first to those community colleges with few middle-class students, just as attractive magnet programs are placed in higher-poverty elementary and secondary schools

Provide Incentives for Four-Year Institutions to Engage in Affirmative Action for Low-Income Students of All Races. There is a great deal of evidence that four-year institutions could do a much better job of attracting "strivers," low-income students who achieve at higher levels than expected given the disadvantages they face. The effort to recruit promising low-income students to four-year institutions is important in its own right. It will provide new opportunities for low-income students, and the greater diversity created will benefit the education of all students. But expanded efforts would also serve as a complement to plans enacted by community colleges to attract more middle-class students by relieving overcrowding at the community college level. In short, breaking down stratification between two- and four-year colleges will require deliberate programs on the part of both sets of institutions.

CONCLUSION

Taken together, we believe these innovations in financing and governance of higher education can dramatically enhance the prospect of millions of students attending our nation's community colleges. The two primary strategies outlined—adequacy-based funding and de-stratification of student populations—go hand in glove.

Efforts to make inequalities in higher education funding more transparent, coupled with legal and public policy efforts to level-up public funding of community colleges, should make it possible to improve the quality of community colleges. Improved quality, in turn, may attract a broader cross-section of students, including those from more-affluent backgrounds. The de-stratification that flows from increased quality, coupled with targeted efforts to de-stratify higher education, should further promote the virtuous cycle. Less stratification should help create political capital to sustain investments in community colleges; and the higher expectations of less-stratified community college populations should help create "transfer cultures" that will improve outcomes for low-income students beyond the benefits associated merely with greater financial resources.

Today, community colleges are in great danger of becoming indelibly separate and unequal institutions in the higher education landscape. As *Brown v. Board of Education* helped galvanize our nation to address deep and enduring inequalities that had long been taken for granted, so today it is time to address—head on—abiding racial and economic inequalities in our system of American higher education. To date, community college reform is mostly about sharing best practices, an important but overly narrow discussion. It is time to take bold action to enhance the role of community colleges in strengthening American competitiveness, bolstering American democracy, and reviving the American Dream.

Report of the Task Force

THE COMMUNITY COLLEGE CHALLENGE

American community colleges stand at the confluence of four mighty rivers that are profoundly influencing all of American life. At a time of growing economic globalization, community colleges are a critical element in the strategy to address the skills and education gap to meet the emerging needs of American industries in the new knowledge economy. At a time of stagnant social mobility, two-year open-access institutions are pivotal in efforts to restore the American Dream. At a time when soaring college costs are putting four-year institutions out of the reach of many students, community colleges remain a relatively affordable option for millions of Americans. And, at a time of deep demographic change that is making obsolete the very term *minority*, community colleges educate nearly half of America's undergraduates of color.[1]

Yet, for reasons outlined below, public community colleges, which serve some 11 million students and 44 percent of the U.S. college population, often are not currently equipped for the challenge.[2] Although many community colleges do a superb job of serving disadvantaged populations, on the whole, the college "dropout" rate for American students may be as high as 50 percent—far higher than the high school dropout rate—and community college dropout rates are higher still.[3] If our nation does not assist community colleges in better serving their students, it will be less economically competitive and poorer. The American Dream will remain out of reach for millions of our fellow citizens. Nonwhite and non-Anglo students, the coming majority, will be left behind. And college will increasingly become a luxury for the wealthy. Because higher education is a public good, not just a private good, we all have a stake in ensuring that everyone receives the best education possible.

It is possible to build a better future: we did it before, in the context of high school educational attainment. As Claudia Golden and Lawrence F. Katz note in *The Race between Education and Technology*, by 1900, the United States, unlike most other countries, had "begun to educate its masses at the secondary level not just in primary schools," and soon became the richest nation in the world.[4] We were once a world leader in the number of young people receiving an associate's degree or higher, but today, the United States ranks fourteenth among OECD nations in terms of percentage of the population ages 25–34 in that category.[5]

Today, community colleges are charged with being both the central vehicle for jumpstarting social mobility in America and a key driver in the efforts to make the country more globally competitive. In striving for the Obama administration's goal of raising postsecondary graduation rates to be first in the world by 2020—so that 60 percent of 25–34 year olds have a postsecondary credential—community colleges are expected to shoulder the bulk of the challenge. Of 8 million new degrees required to reach the goal, the Obama administration expects 5 million (or 63 percent) to come from the community college sector.[6]

Yet, given the way community colleges are currently structured and supported, it is no wonder that many have a difficult time reaching the goals being set for them. A central problem is that two-year colleges are asked to educate those students with the greatest needs, with the least funds, and in increasingly separate and unequal institutions. Our higher education system, like the larger society, is growing more and more unequal.

Although stark divisions between two- and four-year institutions in theory are supposed to produce efficiencies—with each set of institutions focusing on what it does best—under our existing structures, 65 percent of students who begin at a community college fail to earn a degree or certificate from their starting institution or another school within six years.[7] While 81.4 percent of students entering community college for the first time say they eventually want to transfer and earn at least a bachelor's degree, only 11.6 percent of entering community colleges students do so within six years.[8]

The American Association of Community Colleges, the primary advocacy organization for the nation's community colleges, frankly acknowledged in a recent commission report: "What we find today are student success rates that are unacceptably low, employment preparation that is inadequately connected to job market needs and disconnects in transitions between high schools, community colleges, and baccalaureate institutions."[9]

The challenge to improve success rates at community colleges comes at a time of growing austerity and substantial cuts in public support for higher education. Community colleges have borne the brunt of these cuts, according to the Delta Cost Project, and "disparities between rich and poor institutions in overall spending levels have never been larger."[10] Many community colleges are stretched to capacity and are unable to keep up with demand, sending more and more students into the for-profit sector, where students are often poorly served.

Although the challenges are considerable, we have great optimism that if critical innovations are made to the financing and design of community colleges, and if bold changes are undertaken to address the increasing economic and racial isolation of students, two-year colleges can both become more effective and build further their vital role as engines of social mobility and economic competitiveness for students from all backgrounds. In short, they can become America's quintessential "middle-class" institutions—serving both those already in the middle-class and those aspiring to become part of it.

Addressing the Challenges of a Two-Tiered System

In order to address the fundamental challenge, the Task Force believes we must do much more than just share and replicate best practices of successful community colleges—as valuable and important as doing so is. In addition, we need to confront head-on the growing stratification and separation between economic and racial groups in higher education, which results in a system that educates those students with the greatest needs apart from more-advantaged students, and does so with fewer resources. While some differentiation between two- and four-year institutions is appropriate, a rigid, two-tier system, which offers little fluidity between levels, and tends to educate different income and racial and ethnic groups in different settings, is neither inevitable nor desirable, nor, the evidence suggests, particularly efficient.

To be sure, the original two-tier system had many laudable features. The U.S. system of community colleges arose as separate and distinct from the traditional four-year system for several reasons: to broaden access to higher education; to meet the special needs of communities for vocational training and lifelong learning; and to provide an efficient, lower-cost means of educating students in the first two years of college.

Unlike many four-year institutions, community colleges generally do not impose strict entrance requirements and are open to all.[11]

More numerous than four-year institutions, community colleges can be located close to where students reside and work, so students of all ages can live at home and not incur the expense of residential college living. Two-year colleges charge relatively low tuitions and provide flexible scheduling to accommodate student job responsibilities. The community aspect of these colleges allows them to focus on the particular needs of local employers, and to form important partnerships to promote lifelong learning. Community colleges can provide hands-on, job-specific training that often leads to well-paying jobs. And the comparatively lower costs of community colleges to taxpayers was also thought to be an efficient way of educating first- and second-year students, many of whom expected to transfer to four-year institutions after receiving an associate's degree.

All of these distinctive features remain strengths of the community college system, but each of these attractive features has posed profound challenges. Because community colleges are separate institutions, and because they tend to serve more disadvantaged populations, the separate structures and stratified student populations impose costs that should be frankly acknowledged and considered as reforms are proposed.

- Because community colleges have different funding streams than four-year institutions, they lack the resources necessary to accomplish their goals. While policymakers see community colleges as a relatively inexpensive way to educate large numbers of students, the under-resourcing of the system in fact has helped create large inefficiencies, with low completion rates.
- Because community colleges and four-year institutions do not seamlessly connect, the great majority of students who indicate an intention to transfer and receive a bachelor's degree face unnecessary barriers to doing so.
- Because community colleges increasingly serve low-income and working-class student populations, different sets of curricula, expectations, and institutional cultures about transfer have emerged at community colleges that can harm students by setting lower standards and expectations than those at four-year institutions. Furthermore, as the socioeconomic divide between two- and four-year institutions grows, students at community colleges are cut off from valuable middle-class peer networks found at four-year institutions.

A fundamental challenge involves seeing whether there are ways to retain the benefits offered by the unique features of community colleges while reducing the stratification and separation that has generated problems for the sector. To begin with, it is instructive to briefly look at the K–12 system, which has many years of experience addressing large-scale stratification, and then apply the lessons to higher education.

How Some Elementary and Secondary School Policies Seek to Address Stratification

In the K–12 realm, racial and economic stratification has long been recognized as a major impediment to equal opportunity, and policymakers have sought to address the issue by reducing separation (through racial and economic school integration programs) and by providing additional funding to schools with concentrations of poverty. As more and more students go to college, the experience of elementary and secondary schools in addressing stratification becomes more relevant to higher education.

In the landmark *Brown v. Board of Education* decision in 1954, a unanimous U.S. Supreme Court famously recognized that separate schools for black and white children were inherently unequal. Today, social science research suggests that economic segregation in schools is highly detrimental: for any given student, attending a higher-poverty school predicts significantly lower outcomes. While a great deal of media attention is lavished on high-poverty schools that produce positive outcomes for students, these schools are rare. In a 2006 study, University of Wisconsin professor Douglas Harris found that high-poverty schools were twenty-two times less likely to be high-performing than low-poverty schools.[12]

Of course, part of the reason high-poverty schools struggle is that low-income students, on average, come to school less prepared, but data from the National Assessment of Educational Progress (NAEP) elucidates a separate phenomenon connected to school poverty concentrations. In 2011, low-income fourth grade students who attend more-affluent schools scored twenty points higher in mathematics—the equivalent of roughly two years of learning—than low-income students attending high-poverty schools. Indeed, *low-income* students given a chance to attend more-affluent schools performed about half a year better, on average, than *middle-income* students who attend high-poverty schools.[13]

Selection effects may explain some of the superior performance of low-income students in more-affluent schools, but an interesting 2010 Century Foundation study of students in Montgomery County, Maryland, suggests that there are significant advantages to attending lower-poverty schools, even when students are randomly assigned. Heather Schwartz, a researcher at the RAND Corporation, compared students whose families applied for public housing and were randomly assigned to housing units and neighborhood schools in different parts of Montgomery County. Some families were assigned to public housing units in the less-affluent eastern portion of the county, where schools, designated as being in the "Red Zone," were allocated an additional $2,000 per pupil for reduced class size in the early grades, extended learning time, and additional professional development for teachers. Other families were assigned to public housing units in the more-affluent western part of the county, designated as the "Green Zone," which did not receive the extra resources provided in the Red Zone.

After several years, low-income elementary students in the lower-poverty Green Zone schools outperformed low-income students in Red Zone schools by 0.4 of a standard deviation in math, a large effect size among educational interventions.[14] Two-thirds of the positive benefit was associated with schooling, and one-third with neighborhood. Attending schools with lower levels of economic segregation is also associated with improved graduation rates in secondary schooling.[15]

Policymakers have responded with a number of interventions to address problems associated with racial and economic segregation and to remedy the disadvantages associated with poverty. Among the leading strategies have been efforts to attack segregation head-on through inter-district public school choice programs to promote economic and racial school integration; and funding programs to recognize that extra resources are required to provide students from disadvantaged families with equal educational opportunity.

The U.S. Supreme Court allows school districts to employ race as a factor in student assignment under certain circumstances. Moreover, it is perfectly legal to integrate by socioeconomic status, and nationally, more than eighty school districts, educating some 4 million students, deliberately seek to de-stratify school populations by socioeconomic status.[16] Districts employ two basic choice-based strategies to integrate schools: they create "magnet" schools to attract middle-class students into economically disadvantaged schools; and they allow low-income students to transfer to higher-performing middle-class schools. Both sets of strategies are associated with considerably higher achievement for low-income students and no decline in the achievement of middle-class students.[17]

Policymakers have also recognized that not all schools will be socioeconomically and racially integrated, and those public schools with higher concentrations of poverty deserve additional resources. It is widely known that wealthy families are in a position to invest far greater resources in their children outside of school than are low-income families. Research suggests the gap in investment levels has tripled since the 1970s.[18]

In K–12 schooling, considerable research has been conducted on the extra weighted funding appropriate for low-income students in order for them to receive an "adequate" education. A 2008 review of thirteen studies in nine states found that the cost of educating economically disadvantaged students ranged from 22.5 percent to 167.9 percent more than the cost of educating other students.[19] Another review of studies found that estimates of the cost of educating students qualifying for free or reduced-price lunch ranged from 35 percent more to 100 percent more per pupil compared with the cost of educating a non-qualifying student. Most of the estimates fell in the range of 60 percent to 100 percent.[20] While the studies ranged in their conclusions regarding the premium deserved, all agreed extra funds are required to educate more economically disadvantaged students to proficiency.

Federal policy, dating back to the 1965 Elementary and Secondary Education Act, has recognized that children in higher-poverty schools deserve extra resources, and hundreds of billions of dollars in Title I funds have been devoted to providing aid to higher-poverty schools. In part because of litigation on behalf of low-income students, state funding formulas in K–12 education routinely provide additional spending for low-income students. Nationally, more than two-thirds of all states provide additional funding for low-income students or students in need of remedial education, most commonly awarding 25 percent more.[21]

Stratification in Higher Education: An Emerging Issue

The distinction between K–12 and higher education policy on the issue of racial and economic stratification between institutions is striking. Elite higher education has recognized the need to integrate by race, adopting affirmative action programs to enhance the representation of African American and Latino students, but there has been no comparable effort to integrate by socioeconomic status.[22] And there is little deliberate effort to draw more middle- and upper-middle-class students to community colleges, as "magnet schools" work to do at the K–12 level. Likewise, as is outlined below, there is no comparable effort to provide extra federal and state resources to community colleges analogous to federal Title I funding or state-level adequacy funding at the K–12 level. Despite the progressive features of the Pell Grant program, state and federal resources tilt overall toward colleges with more advantaged student populations.

On one level, it is understandable that higher education has been slow to address issues of stratification. While primary and secondary schools have long educated a broad cross section of the American public, the entire higher education sector was fairly elite until recently. In the early 1950s, around the time *Brown v. Board of Education* was decided, only 6.9 percent of Americans aged 25 years or older had a four-year college degree, and another 7.6 percent had one to three years of college.[23] With only 14.5 percent of the adult population falling into these categories, issues of stratification between higher education institutions was not particularly salient. Two-year colleges were a minor player. As late as 1965, only one-quarter of public college students were in community colleges.[24]

Today, however, stratification issues loom much larger. Paradoxically, as Anthony P. Carnevale and Jeff Strohl have observed, increasing college access is increasing inequality within the higher education universe.[25] In 2011, more than half (53.9 percent) of Americans aged 25 years or older had at either a four-year degree or more (32.1 percent) or one to three years of college (21.8 percent), almost four times the share in the early 1950s—making issues of who goes where far more important.[26]

Figure 1 vividly illustrates the socioeconomic breakdown of students in community colleges compared with four-year institutions of varying levels of selectivity. In 2006, high-SES students outnumbered low-SES students by 14 to 1 in the most competitive four-year institutions, yet low-SES students outnumbered high-SES students in community colleges by nearly 2 to 1.

Racial and ethnic stratification is also striking. At the most selective four-year colleges in 2006, whites constituted 75 percent of students, and blacks and Hispanics together totaled 12 percent of students. In community colleges, by contrast, whites accounted for 58 percent of students, and blacks and Latinos together totaled 33 percent of students.[27] Parallel patterns can be found in 2010 data comparing student populations at two-year public and four-year institutions more generally.[28] Moreover, although the aggregated community college population is

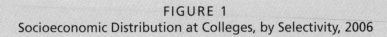

FIGURE 1
Socioeconomic Distribution at Colleges, by Selectivity, 2006

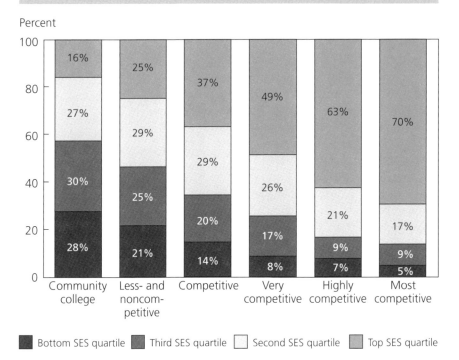

Percent

| | Community college | Less- and noncompetitive | Competitive | Very competitive | Highly competitive | Most competitive |

Bottom SES quartile   Third SES quartile   Second SES quartile   Top SES quartile

Note: Some columns do not total 100 due to rounding.
Source: Anthony P. Carnevale and Jeff Strohl, "How Increasing College Access Is Increasing Inequality, and What to Do about It," in *Rewarding Strivers: Helping Low-Income Students Succeed in College,* ed. Richard D. Kahlenberg (New York: Century Foundation Press, 2010), 137, Figure 3.7.

diverse, research conducted for the Task Force by Sara Goldrick-Rab and Peter Kinsley shows that many individual community colleges have levels of segregation for minority students that are as high if not higher than those at the most elite institutions for white students. When broken down into quartiles of underrepresented minority populations, the most racially isolated quarter of community colleges have student bodies in which almost two-thirds of students are from underrepresented minority groups.[29]

Moreover, socioeconomic and racial and ethnic stratification has grown, not lessened, in recent decades. In 1982, students from the top socioeconomic quarter of the population made up 24 percent of the students at community colleges; by 2006, that had dropped to 16 percent.

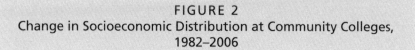

FIGURE 2
**Change in Socioeconomic Distribution at Community Colleges,
1982–2006**

Percent

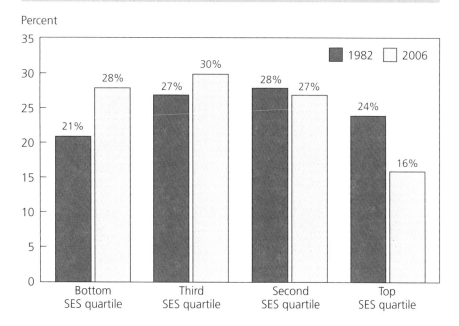

Source: Anthony P. Carnevale and Jeff Strohl, "How Increasing College Access Is Increasing Inequality, and What to Do about It," in *Rewarding Strivers: Helping Low-Income Students Succeed in College,* ed. Richard D. Kahlenberg (New York: Century Foundation Press, 2010), 136–37, Figures 3.6 and 3.7.

Conversely, the representation of the poorest quarter of the population has grown at community colleges from 21 percent to 28 percent in the same time period.[30] (See Figure 2.)

The change in racial and ethnic makeup also shows interesting patterns. Between 1994 and 2006, the white share of the community college population plummeted from 73 percent to 58 percent, while black and Hispanic representation grew from 21 percent to 33 percent, in part reflecting growing diversity in the population as a whole. By contrast, the change was much less dramatic at the most selective four-year colleges during this time period, when the white share dipped just three percentage points (from 78 percent to 75 percent) and the black and Hispanic shares barely moved (from 11 percent to 12 percent).[31]

Some press stories suggest that the recession has brought a flood of upper-middle-class students into community colleges, but the report on which these stories are based depicts a different story. In the years since 2007, tough economic times have indeed brought an influx of students from all economic groups to community colleges, but low-income students have actually increased their use of two-year institutions at a far faster pace than either middle-income or high-income students.[32]

Why Economic and Racial Stratification Matters

The increasing economic and racial stratification of colleges and universities is troubling because largely separate educational systems for mostly rich and white students, and for mostly poor and minority students are rarely equal. As the evidence below suggests, racial and economic stratification is connected to unequal financial resources as well as unequal curriculum, expectations, and school cultures.[33]

Stratification and Financial Resources. The stratified student populations in higher education put community colleges, which educate disproportionate shares of low-income and working-class students, at a double disadvantage with respect to funding. On the one hand, disadvantaged students generally have greater educational needs and need additional resources to reach a given level of proficiency. On the other hand, low-income and working-class people generally wield less political power in our political system and institutions serving them are often short-changed on resources. This double bind plays out clearly with respect to the funding of community colleges.

Community college students, on average, come to higher education further behind and have greater education needs compared with their more highly prepared counterparts at four-year institutions. While there do not appear to be extensive studies quantifying the premiums required for low-income and working-class students in higher education the way there are in the K–12 arena (an issue we take up in our recommendations) it seems reasonable to suspect that the needs of the average community college student are greater than more academically advanced students typically found in four-year institutions. We do know, for example, that more than 60 percent of community college students receive some developmental/remedial education, at an estimated cost of $2 billion per year.[34]

Although they arguably serve students with greater needs, community colleges spend far less per pupil than four-year institutions. As Figure 3 indicates (page 22), per-pupil total operating expenditures in academic

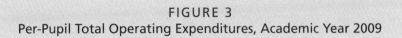

FIGURE 3
Per-Pupil Total Operating Expenditures, Academic Year 2009

Spending per FTE student (in 2009 dollars)

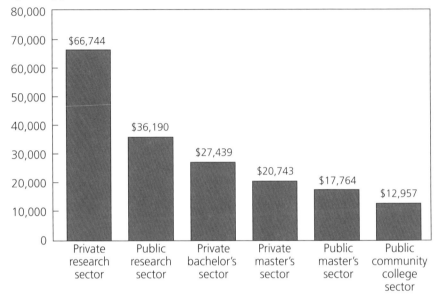

Source: Donna M. Desrochers and Jane V. Wellman, *Trends in College Spending 1999–2009* (Washington, D.C.: Delta Project on Postsecondary Education Costs, Productivity, and Accountability, 2011), figure A2, 52–57, http://www.deltacostproject.org/resources/pdf/Trends2011_Final_090711.pdf.

year 2009 were far lower for community colleges (about $13,000 per full-time equivalent student) compared with various four-year institutions. Total operating expenditures are five times higher for private research universities than community colleges, on average.

Moreover, evidence suggests that the per-pupil total operating expenditures gap has grown over time. As Figure 4 demonstrates, between academic years 1999 and 2009, every four-year sector saw increases, while community college funding was flat. During this ten-year period, at the extremes, private research sector expenditures increased by $13,912, while public community colleges saw a rise of just $1 (expressed in 2009 dollars).

Of course, four-year research institutions are charged not only with educating students, but also with advancing human knowledge, whereas community colleges are primarily teaching institutions. But even when

FIGURE 4
Change in Per-Pupil Total Operating Expenditures,
Academic Year 1999–2009

Ten-year change in spending per FTE student (in 2009 dollars)

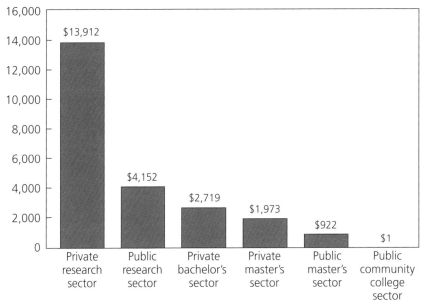

Source: Donna M. Desrochers and Jane V. Wellman, *Trends in College Spending 1999–2009* (Washington, D.C.: Delta Project on Postsecondary Education Costs, Productivity, and Accountability, 2011), figure A2, 52–57, http://www.deltacostproject.org/resources/pdf/Trends2011_Final_090711.pdf.

sponsored research and spending on auxiliary enterprises (such as hospitals) are excluded, the per-pupil spending is far lower at public community colleges ($10,242) than at various four-year institutions (ranging from $12,363 to $35,596), as Figure 5 shows (page 24). Likewise, focusing exclusively on "instruction" expenses, community colleges spent about $5,000 per pupil in 2009, compared with $10,000 at public research universities and $20,000 at private research universities.[35] (For further discussion see Box 1, page 26.)

To be sure, community college students pay significantly less in tuition and fees than students at most four-year institutions, but community college tuition levels have risen dramatically as a share of revenues in the past two decades as state and local appropriations have declined.[36] This increasing reliance on tuition fees is highly problematic

FIGURE 5
Per-Pupil Education and Related Spending, Academic Year 2009
(i.e., excluding sponsored research and auxiliary enterprises)

Spending per FTE student (in 2009 dollars)

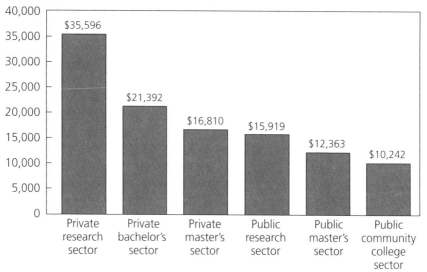

Note: Education and related expenses (E&R) is a measure of institutional spending that excludes spending on auxiliary enterprises (such as hospitals) and sponsored research. Desrochers and Wellman explain the rationale behind this calculation: "E&R offers the most robust measure of spending on student learning because it isolates spending related to the education mission. E&R includes spending on instruction, student services, and a portion of general support and maintenance costs associated with these functions. Some analysts refer to this as a 'full cost' measure, distinct from measures of 'direct instructional' costs, which account for faculty salaries but exclude everything else. Because it includes spending for faculty salaries (except those paid from research contracts), E&R also includes spending for departmental or non-sponsored research. While some would prefer to exclude all research costs from E&R spending, it is a mission-related instructional cost in research institutions, as is the cost of graduate education, and so we will include it within the measure" (20).
Source: Donna M. Desrochers and Jane V. Wellman, *Trends in College Spending 1999–2009* (Washington, D.C.: Delta Project on Postsecondary Education Costs, Productivity, and Accountability, 2011), figure A2, 52–57, http://www.deltacostproject.org/resources/pdf/Trends2011_Final_090711.pdf.

given the role of two-year colleges in providing access to low-income and working-class students. Moreover, even when one isolates per-pupil public subsidies in the form of state and local appropriations, federal appropriations, and federal, state, and local grants and contracts, public community colleges fare poorly compared with public research sector institutions (see Figure 6). Community colleges are roughly on par with public master's sector institutions.

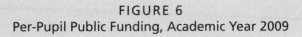

FIGURE 6
Per-Pupil Public Funding, Academic Year 2009

Revenues per FTE student (in 2009 dollars)

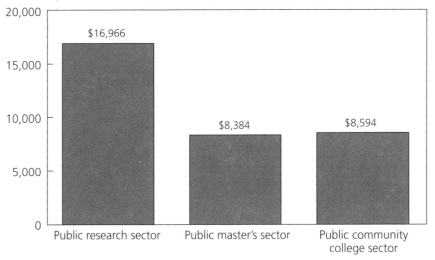

Note: Public funding includes state and local appropriations; federal appropriations; and federal, state, and local grants and contracts.
Source: Donna M. Desrochers and Jane V. Wellman, *Trends in College Spending 1999–2009* (Washington, D.C.: Delta Project on Postsecondary Education Costs, Productivity, and Accountability, 2011), figure A1, 48–51, http://www.deltacostproject.org/resources/pdf/Trends2011_Final_090711.pdf.

Less transparent is the public assistance to private research institutions in the form of numerous tax subsidies. Government tax expenditures take several forms, including the ability of donors to deduct donations from taxable income, and the tax-free status of endowment income. When a wealthy individual donates a library or dormitory to a private institution, for example, it is likely that the public indirectly pays one-third of the cost in the form of lost tax revenue. One economist suggests the tax and research subsidies for a private university can run as high a $54,000 per student compared with just $600 per student at a nearby public institution.[37]

Nationally, the tax expenditures for higher education are considerable. According to a 2007 analysis by the Congressional Research Service, the foregone income tax revenue for some 765 nonprofit colleges with accumulated endowments of $340 billion cost the government $18 billion. With more modest returns in recent years, Sandy Baum

---

BOX 1
Complications in Comparing the Expenditures
of Two- and Four-Year Institutions

Even after excluding research expenses, there are important nuances to be recognized in comparing funding of two- and four-year colleges as is outlined in the background paper for this task force prepared by Sandy Baum and Charles Kurose. On the one hand, community colleges might expect to need lower amounts of funding because the first two years of college are generally less expensive to teach than the third and fourth years.* On the other hand, there are countervailing considerations surrounding the difference between two- and four -year institutions suggesting that from an equity standpoint, community colleges require greater funding. First- and second-year students in four-year institutions may be more amenable to being educated in large lecture halls because they are more likely to be well-prepared academically, whereas community college students may require smaller class sizes given their levels of preparation.** Likewise, vocational education provided in community college setting can be fairly expensive, requiring a greater devotion of resources.*** Finally, given the reality that only about 10 percent of community college students persist to a bachelor's degree, benefiting from four full years of public subsidies, allowances might be made for community college students on whom far fewer resources are likely to be showered over the long haul.

*Jane Wellman, "Financial Characteristics of broad access public institutions," Background paper prepared for the Stanford Conference on Mapping Broad Access Higher Education, December 1–2, 2011, 3–4 and 12.
**Ibid., 23.
***Ibid., 13–14.

---

and Charles Kurose put the annual cost at $6.2 billion. Meanwhile, the deduction for charitable contributions for educational institutions cost an estimated $6.6 billion in 2007. Nonprofit colleges are also exempt from property taxes and sales taxes, though the amount of this subsidy is hard to quantify.[38]

Public community colleges benefit from very few of these tax expenditures. In 2007, public community college derived just $372 per full time equivalent student from private and affiliated gifts, grants, contracts, investment returns, and endowment income. By contrast, private bachelor's institutions derived $20,035 per pupil from such sources, and private research institutions derived $46,342 per pupil.[39] As one community college president remarked: wealthy hedge fund managers give to their own colleges, and fund charter schools for low-income students, but rarely do they adopt a community college.

Overall, then, higher education appears to operate on something like the reverse of the "adequacy" model in K–12 education, where federal and state resources flow disproportionately to students most in need. While significant federal programs do exist to provide grant aid to economically disadvantaged student, most prominently in the form of Pell Grants, the program ends up bypassing many low-income community college students, for whom tuition and fees are low and the primary expense of attending college is the opportunity costs associated with forgone wages. And the progressive element of Pell funding is heavily diluted by numerous state and institutional "merit aid" programs as well as poorly targeted federal tax breaks for education expenses that can benefit students from families making up to $180,000 a year.[40] Moreover, whereas the bulk of direct federal grants to elementary and secondary schools use a relatively progressive funding formula under Title I of the Elementary and Secondary Education Act that is meant to benefit schools with concentrations of low-income students, the Brookings Institution reports that direct federal aid to higher education disproportionately benefits four-year over two-year institutions. The authors of a 2009 Brookings policy brief note, "four-year institutions receive nearly three times as much in federal support per full-time equivalent (FTE) student ($2,650) as community colleges ($790)."[41] The Brookings report noted that direct federal support for community colleges stood at $2 billion annually, a very modest commitment in comparison to the $20 billion a year allocated to public four-year universities and $60 billion a year spent on K–12 education.[42]

The current underfunding of community colleges may well be connected to the political realities of who holds power in American society. As we noted above, students from the upper quartile in socioeconomic status are under-represented at community colleges, and have become increasingly so in recent decades. Community colleges will always have local employers who provide political support for funding, but the decline in middle- and upper-middle-class representation in the sector may, over the long haul, weaken support for strong funding of two-year institutions. One early illustration of this vulnerability came in 2010, when the Obama administration's 2009 proposal for $12 billion in new community college funding was trimmed by a Democratic Congress to just $2 billion. Likewise, a $5 billion proposal to fund infrastructure at community colleges in September 2011 and an $8 billion proposal to fund a Community College to Career Fund in February 2012 have seen no congressional action.[43] Cuts to community colleges have not seemed to generate the political backlash, or the media attention, that issues such as a slated increase in the interest rate for student loans—which affects students across sectors—have generated. Although community colleges educate very large numbers of students, and are geographically disbursed into different legislative and congressional districts, it appears that the focus on lower-income and working class students—the crowning glory of the two-year sector—also presents a political liability when it comes to funding.

As noted in the recommendations set forth below, we do not believe that higher education funding should be considered a zero sum game, in which funds now used at four-year institutions should be diverted to community colleges. We do not call for a reduction in tax subsidies for four-year institutions, which are a vital national resource deserving of continued support. We do, however, believe that efforts should be made to level-up investment in two-year colleges to provide them with the resources necessary to provide an excellent education.

How Social Composition Influences Curriculum, Expectations, and School Culture. If socioeconomic and racial stratification between two-year and four-year institutions puts community colleges at a double funding disadvantage (educating students with the greatest needs, but the least political power), there are additional reasons to believe stratification is problematic above and beyond the question of funding. In discussing why, controlling for demographic and academic qualifications, individual students are more likely to succeed in more selective institutions, William Bowen and colleagues cite not only access to superior financial resources, but also aspects such as valuable peer networks and school cultures with high expectations. On the issue of peers, Bowen and colleagues write: "Students learn from each other. Being surrounded by highly capable classmates improves the learning environment and promotes good educational outcomes of all kinds, including timely graduation." With respect to expectations, Bowen and company suggest: "The high overall graduation rates at the most selective public universities unquestionably create a climate in which graduating, and graduating with one's class, are compelling norms. Students feel pressure to keep pace with their classmates."[44]

Likewise, Richard Arum and Josipa Roksa's research in their book *Academically Adrift* finds that "Being surrounded by peers who are well prepared for college-level work is likely to shape the climate of the institution as well as specific student experiences. Having high-performing students in the classroom can help improve achievement of all students, including those who have accumulated fewer skills before college."[45] Indeed, an academic literature dating back for decades has found benefits associated with positive peer norms not only in K–12 education but in four-year colleges. Researchers Barbara Bank, Ricky Slavins, and Bruce Biddle, for example, found in a longitudinal study at a large Midwestern state university in 1990 that peer norms (though not behaviors) had significant effects on students' college persistence. (Researchers measured peer norms by student survey responses describing the views of their two closest friends.)[46] Accordingly, low-income and working-class students in community colleges who are isolated from those students who are most likely to be high achieving and complete a BA may be placed at a disadvantage.

Having said all this, it is hard to know how an academic literature regarding peer effects at four-year residential institutions applies to community college settings, where most students commute to campus. Likewise, unlike the K–12 setting, community college classrooms often have students from a wide range of ages. Peer effects may be stronger in a room full of 15- or 20-year-olds than in a classroom with 19-year-old, 32-year-old and 49-year-old students. We need to be cautious, then, about the role of peer effects in community colleges, but also cognizant of their potential power.

Applying the findings on peer effects to community colleges, Columbia University's Juan Carlos Calcagno, Thomas Bailey, and others made this observation:

> Research on peer effects suggests that college students benefit when they take classes with or study with high-performing students, but most of this work has focused on selective 4-year colleges. Assuming that this conclusion holds for community colleges, we would expect that colleges with high proportions of women, higher income students, and full-time students would have higher graduation rates, even after controlling for individual characteristics, since members [of] all of these groups tend to be more successful students.[47]

Being around well-connected peers may also increase a student's chances of employment success, apart from any impact on academic outcomes.

Student body composition also appears to affect curriculum offerings, at least in part. As low-income and working-class students have become an increasing share of the student bodies at community colleges, researchers have found that institutions have focused more and more on a vocational curriculum leading to certificates rather than a liberal arts curriculum preparing students to transfer to four-year institutions.[48] On one level, this trend is understandable: schools often have higher completion rates in certificate programs than in those geared toward an associate's degree and transfer, and many students feel the need to receive training for a job they can start today rather than pursuing a full degree in the future.[49] Moreover, taking courses and earning degrees in quantitative or technical areas can have higher marketplace returns than those in fields such as the social sciences or humanities.[50] At the same time, community college students in working-class settings that do not have a culture of transfer may find themselves steered by the curriculum to certificates in technical fields whether or not they wish to pursue that path. And research finds some—though not all—community colleges can be marked by "low expectations of teachers and lack of support from fellow students for academic work."[51]

Evidence that Racial and Economic Stratification— and the Reduced Resources Associated with Stratification— May Reduce Outcomes for Low-Income and Minority Students

With fewer financial resources and often a different curriculum and set of expectations, schools that are racially and economically isolated sometimes produce poor results. In the K–12 arena, there is ample evidence that racial and economic stratification can have a negative impact on student outcomes, as we outlined earlier. Considerable evidence suggests that we should be similarly concerned about the growing economic and racial divide in higher education.

To begin with, the raw data suggest students are generally more successful in four-year colleges than community colleges. According to data from the 2004/2009 Beginning Postsecondary Students Longitudinal Study (BPS), only 34.5 percent of students who started in a two-year college earned a degree or certificate (from their starting institution or another school) within six years (8.5 percent earned certificates, 14.4 percent earned associate's degrees, and 11.6 percent earned bachelor's degrees).[52] By contrast, 57 percent of first-time students enrolled in bachelor's programs or equivalents at four-year institutions earned bachelor's degrees within six years.[53]

The relatively poor results in community colleges are surely in part a reflection of selection effects, given that individual students come to community college less prepared on average. Moreover, even studies that control for preparation and demographic characteristics broadly may miss additional disadvantages that community college students face disproportionately. For example, a student may select to attend a local community college rather than a four-year institution because she is working to support a multigenerational household or is caring for a family member with a mental illness that makes it difficult to attend a four-year residential institution. Still, considerable research finds that where one goes to college has an independent effect on outcomes—and that attending schools with more affluent student bodies (and greater resources) can have a positive effect. (We recognize that data from the Integrated Postsecondary Education Data System [IPEDS] are flawed with respect to community college graduation rates, as outlined in the Appendix, and recommend that improvements be made in the future.)

Diminished Outcomes at Community Colleges. For one thing, researchers have documented a reduction in the chances of ultimately earning a bachelor's degree associated with a given individual attending a community college as compared with a four-year institution, controlling for a student's level of preparation. For example, among low-income students with "high" qualifications for college (those who have completed "at least Trigonometry"), 69 percent of students who began in a four-year institution earned a bachelor's degree, compared with just 19 percent of those who started in a community college.[54]

The trigonometry metric may not fully capture selection effects within the universe of students who have completed the course, but other careful studies have sought to address selection bias. In a 2006 study, using a nationally representative sample of students and controlling for relevant characteristics, C. Lockwood Reynolds, an economist now at Kent State University, estimated that beginning at a two-year college reduces one's chances of ultimately receiving a bachelor's degree by 30 percentage points.[55] William Bowen and colleagues, analyzing North Carolina data in their 2007 book, *Crossing the Finish Line,* also report reduced outcomes after controlling for academic preparation and demographic factors such as gender, family income, parental education, and educational aspirations. For example, among white students with high grade point averages and SAT scores of about 1200, bachelor's degree attainment rates were 36 points higher (47 percent versus 83 percent) if they began at a four-year institution. Among whites with lower credentials (lower grades and SAT scores of about 800), the gap was about 29 points. Among black students, baccalaureate attainment decreased when they attended a community college instead of a four-year institution (whether predominantly white or historically black).[56] Likewise, in a 2008 paper for the National Bureau of Economic Research, Bridget Terry Long of Harvard University and Michal Kurlaender of U.C. Davis conclude that after carefully controlling for selection bias, students who initially began at a community college in Ohio were conservatively estimated to be 14.5 percent less likely to complete a bachelor's degree within nine years.[57]

A forthcoming study by the Georgetown University Center on Education and the Workforce found that a student who initially enrolled at a public community college on average completes 1.62 fewer years of schooling. After controlling for a host of individual student factors (family income, higher education level of one's parents, race, ethnicity, age of student, grades in high school, whether one received a traditional high school degree, whether the student works full time, and whether the student enrolls in college full time), the gap declines to 0.76 years. The authors suggest the residual difference could reflect the fact that community colleges spend less per full time equivalent student and provide less advantageous peer environments.[58]

To be clear, the research does not suggest that these diminished outcomes are the result of anything inherently wrong with two-year institutions. As the evidence above suggests, community colleges must contend with the powerful effects of racial and economic stratification and inadequate funding. These inequities are not inevitable, and there is reason to believe that if they are remedied, it will be possible to elevate outcomes for students in the two-year sector.

Undermatching within Four-Year Institutions. A parallel body of literature finds that within the universe of four-year institutions, a given student is less likely to graduate when she attends a less selective college or university (institutions that also tend to have less affluent student bodies and fewer financial resources). Controlling for preparation levels (and looking at students who would have been presumptively admitted to selective public institutions), former Princeton University president William Bowen, Brookings scholar Matthew Chingos, and Spencer Foundation president Michael McPherson found that attending a less selective four-year institution was associated with a graduation rate of 15 points lower after 6 years (66 percent versus 81 percent). When more sophisticated controls were added, including race, socioeconomic status, and gender, a substantial 10-percentage-point difference remained, and completion times were longer. "In short," they concluded, "the under-matched students paid a considerable price in terms of the time it took them to complete their program of studies and in the reduced probability that they would finish at all."[59]

Evidence from within the Community College Sector. Finally, there is some evidence from within the universe of two-year colleges that racial and socioeconomic composition can affect the performance of any given student. A 2012 study conducted by Mary Martinez-Wenzl and Rigoberto Marquez for the Civil Rights Project of UCLA, for example, found that African American and Latino students in fifty-one Southern California community colleges were more likely to transfer to four-year institutions from high-transfer community colleges (which were all majority white/Asian) than their counterparts in more racially isolated institutions.[60]

In addition, a new background paper prepared for this Task Force provides reason to believe that economic and racial isolation of poor and minority students in community colleges can negatively affect outcomes. The study, conducted by Tatiana Melguizo and Holly Kosiewicz of the University of Southern California, examined student success at more than one hundred community colleges in California, which enroll almost one-quarter of community college students nationally.[61] The authors examine whether the racial and ethnic composition of the student body and the socioeconomic status of the colleges were associated with differences in success. Success was measured by the Student Progress and Achievement Rate (SPAR), a composite measure created by community college leaders that considers such factors as transfers to four-year colleges, AA or AS degrees awarded, and certificates awarded per cohort of students six years after entering.[62]

The sample included a wide variety of institutions, ranging from 11.8 percent underrepresented minority to 90.9 percent. The colleges' socioeconomic status (as measured by the median family income of the location surrounding the community college) ranged from $29,221 to $157,995. During the period considered, SPAR rates ranged from 26.9 to 70.7, with an average of 52.2.[63]

Using institutional level data and controlling for a number of factors, including incoming academic preparation (as measured by the average Academic Performance Index [API] of high schools that feed into each community college and number of students placed in developmental education for math), the authors conclude that having large shares of underrepresented minority students is negatively associated with SPAR,

while having a higher socioeconomic status in the college area is positively associated with SPAR.[64]

In particular, Melguizo and Kosiewicz find that holding all else constant (including academic preparation levels), students in the most-minor-
ity-isolated colleges (those with more than 49 percent underrepresented
minorities) had SPAR scores that were 10 percent lower than students in
colleges with the least-minority-isolated environments (less than 22 percent underrepresented minority.) Likewise, holding all else constant, students in the poorest schools (median area income of less than $50,784)
had SPAR scores that were 8 percent lower than students in the wealthiest schools (median area income of more than $81,718). These results
were statistically significant.[65]

Interestingly, the authors found no association between state and local
funding and SPAR so differences in SPAR rates connected to minority
and low-income student isolation cannot be explained solely by funding differences.[66] The authors conclude, "policymakers should consider
ways to remedy the impact of economic and racial isolation at American
community colleges."[67]

Having said that, a second background paper prepared for this Task
Force by Sara Goldrick-Rab and Peter Kinsley may help explain why
minority racial isolation is associated with reduced outcomes for students in terms of resources provided.

Goldrick-Rab and Kinsley's data provide some evidence that heavily
minority community colleges have fewer resources than predominantly
white community colleges. For example, heavily minority schools (those
with a mean proportion of black, Latino, and Native American students
of 65 percent) have one support staff member for every 294 students,
compared with one support staff for every 85 students in heavily white
and Asian schools (where the mean proportion of underrepresented
minority students is 8 percent).[68] Predominantly white and Asian schools
are also twice as likely to have on-campus housing as predominantly
African American, Latino, and Native American schools (29 percent
versus 15 percent) and twice as likely to have a meal plan (25 percent
versus 13 percent). Predominantly white and Asian schools have lower
student-to-faculty ratios (19 to 1) than those that are predominantly
minority (24 to 1). On the other hand, average nine-month instructional
staff salaries are higher in heavily minority schools ($60,527) than in
predominantly white and Asian schools ($52,843).[69]

The studies conducted by the Civil Rights Project and Melguizo
and Kosiewicz did not control for individual student self-selection, but

research that does seek to control for a number of individual student factors also has found that attending more racially segregated community colleges has a negative effect on student outcomes. A 2008 study in *Economics of Education Review* by Columbia University's Juan Carlos Calcagno, Thomas Bailey, and others examined a national database to see which institutional factors were correlated with attainment outcomes for students and found that, after controlling for the race, test scores and socioeconomic status of individual students, being in a community college with a larger share of minority students predicted lower attainment. Of the multiple factors assessed, minority share, large student populations, and high proportion of part-time faculty were all negatively correlated with student outcomes.[70]

Replicating Inequality. Taking these studies together, it appears that segregation between two- and four-year institutions—and among community colleges—is replicating inequality of opportunity from the K–12 level. Just as white and middle-class flight from urban schools leaves low-income and minority students in low-performing segregated institutions, so higher education reinforces separation and inequality, as community colleges for the most part reflect America's residential segregation. In fact, background research for this Task Force conducted by Sara Goldrick-Rab and Peter Kinsley finds that "more than three-quarters of the variation in racial composition among community colleges is directly attributable to the racial composition of their surrounding geographic locales"[71] In the one-quarter of community colleges where roughly two-thirds of students are underrepresented minorities, much of this segregation can be accounted for by residential status. Unlike many Historically Black Colleges and Universities or Hispanic Serving Institutions, which minority students actively seek out, the demographics of segregated community colleges may be more likely to reflect residential segregation than an affirmative choice on the part of individual students.

Stratification and Inadequate Funding Are Inefficient

The theoretical justification for our stratified system of higher education with differing levels of funding is that it allows different institutions to focus on what they do best. Four-year institutions will cater to the most highly prepared students, the theory suggests, and two-year institutions will educate large numbers of less prepared students to their own levels of success. If our K–12 system and larger society produce a graduating high school population in which low-income students end up less academically prepared than higher-income students, it may be unfortunate. But some would say our system basically works well because we devote more resources to the more talented students and offer a less expensive education to the masses, providing them with an education that is tailored to their particular needs, which in many cases will involve vocational training. This line of argument suggests that efforts to strengthen the connections between two- and four-year institutions are problematic because they involve "mission creep"; instead, the two segments of American higher education should be separate and focus on what they each do best.

But the evidence suggests that a regimented system with clear divisions of duties that attempts to educate community college students on the cheap is neither equitable nor efficient. As noted above, the sharp segmentation between two- and four-year institutions increases the chances that students will "undermatch," which reduces their chances of success. The separation of two- and four-year campuses makes transfers difficult, leaving many talented students without bachelor's degrees. More generally, the underfunding of community colleges, which is meant to educate very large numbers of students inexpensively, in fact may explain extremely high failure rates. While the relatively inexpensive public subsidies provided to community colleges may appear to give taxpayers a good deal, in fact, careful research on the cost per degree shows that trying to educate on the cheap does not work well. When one factors in huge attrition rates, the cost per degree at community colleges is actually more, not less, than at four-year institutions. According to the Delta Cost Project, the spending per degree at public community colleges in 2009 was $73,940, compared with $65,632 at public research institutions and $55,358 at public master's institutions.[72] Mark Schneider finds that the federal, state, and local taxpayers pay $4 billion annually to educate first-year full-time community college students who drop out, though others suggest that figure may be too high.[73]

These findings do not suggest we should disinvest from community colleges, but rather that we should think about ways to decrease inefficiencies (some of which are connected to stratification), consider important redesigns of community colleges to improve effectiveness, and invest wisely in those areas that research suggests make a difference. To illustrate, what follows are four examples of ways in which adequate investment would likely produce positive outcomes in community colleges that would raise overall levels of efficiency.

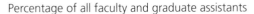

FIGURE 7
Full-time vs. Part-time Faculty, Academic Year 2008

Percentage of all faculty and graduate assistants

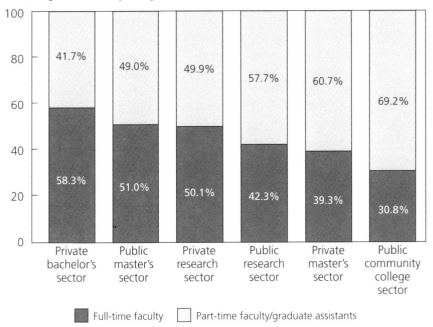

Source: Donna M. Desrochers and Jane V. Wellman, *Trends in College Spending 1999–2009* (Washington, D.C.: Delta Project on Postsecondary Education Costs, Productivity, and Accountability, 2011), 30, http://www.deltacostproject.org/resources/pdf/Trends2011_Final_090711.pdf.

First, there is evidence that being taught by part-time faculty is associated with negative outcomes for students, perhaps because adjunct faculty do not have the same substantive connection to the institution that full-time faculty do.[74] And yet, as a cost saving measure, community colleges rely especially heavily on part time-faculty, as Figure 7 suggests.

Second, community college students face higher student-to-faculty ratios (22-to-1) compared with public four-year students (15-to-1). This translates into larger class sizes and higher course loads for faculty members, which reduces their ability to care for students. Looking at student to all-staff ratios, public two-year students have only half the support (10 to 1) as public four-year students (5 to 1).[75] This lack of support is particularly troubling to the extent that low-income and working-class students often found in community colleges may be in special need for student services (including child care and mental health), and of academic support functions (such as math and writing centers). It is possible that access to tutorials and smaller class size may be a good investment for at-risk students in community college settings. Investing in more advisers and better professional development for faculty could also prove to be wise investments that boost completion rates at a relatively modest cost, thereby reducing cost per degree.[76]

Third, the underinvestment in community colleges has resulted in overcrowding, which diverts many students to for-profit colleges that end up costing students—and taxpayers—much more, with little to show for it. After a two-year investigation of thirty for-profit companies, the U.S. Senate Committee on Health, Education, Labor, and Pensions reported in 2012 that while community colleges and for-profit two-year programs have similar retention rates, "the cost of the for-profit programs makes those programs more risky for students and Federal taxpayers." The report, *For Profit Higher Education: The Failure to Safeguard the Federal Investment and Ensure Student Success*, noted that "For-profit colleges are much more expensive than community colleges, forcing more for-profit students to borrow, and to borrow higher amounts. While 96 percent of those attending a for-profit college borrow to attend, just 13 percent of community college students do so."[77]

Fourth, community colleges should supplement targeted investments with smart reforms of the ways in which education is delivered. The American Association of Colleges and Universities has documented a series of "high impact practices" that increase the likelihood of students progressing towards degrees.[78] Community colleges have also formed consortia and partnerships throughout the country to redesign curriculum and instructional delivery. For example, to improve developmental math instruction in community colleges, the Carnegie Foundation for the Advancement of Teaching has partnered with a consortium of thirty community colleges.[79] Greater investments will be far more effective if they are coupled with these types of curricular redesign.

RECOMMENDATIONS FOR CHANGE

The challenges outlined above lead us to support two major sets of innovations in the financing and governance of higher education. Although most policymakers and institutional leaders focus on highlighting, sharing, and scaling best practices at successful community colleges—something we support—we need to go beyond that limited approach and offer bold and innovative thinking that is also efficacious. In particular, our two central recommendations suggest ways (1) to create a new manner of funding higher education, with a much greater emphasis on providing additional public supports based on student needs; and (2) to reduce the racial and economic stratification between two- and four-year institutions. These recommendations are for federal policymakers, state legislators, foundation heads, and higher education institutional leaders. The central recommendations are guided by our belief in equal opportunity as the goal and incentives rather than compulsion as the means.

Innovations in Funding

In order to make funding more equitable and to provide community colleges with the resources necessary to boost completion (and thereby raise overall efficiency), we recommend the following innovations.

Adopt State and Federal "Adequacy"-Based Funding in Higher Education Akin to that Used in Primary and Secondary Education, Combined with Considerations of Outcomes. We propose greater funding in higher education for institutions serving those students with the greatest needs, tied to accountability for outcomes. We recognize that the current system of funding is inequitable but also acknowledge that the American public has little appetite to pay more for something that is not currently working well.

To begin with, we believe that state and federal funding formulas for higher education should incorporate the concept of "adequacy" funding routinely used at the K–12 level, where extra funds flow to economically disadvantaged students who, on average, have greater educational needs. The current higher education funding system—which provides the two-year sector, educating students with disproportionately greater needs, with fewer funds—should be modernized to align with both state and federal policies at the K–12 level, which provide additional funds to the neediest students. In short, we need a K–12 Title I-type program for higher education.

As part of this effort, we believe the U.S. Education Department should commission a rigorous study of how much more colleges educating disadvantaged students should be provided compared with their peers. (A 25 percent premium is common at the state K–12 level.) One possible methodology would involve examining successful boutique programs providing extra support services, and seeing how much more they cost than typical programs. In assessing the costs of an "adequate" education in the college setting, researchers would recognize that the "goal posts" may be different depending on the educational setting. Whereas states identify uniform standards of "proficiency" for students at the K–12 level, against which adequacy funding is measured, at the postsecondary level, an "adequate" education for a first-year college students may differ depending on whether she is seeking a certificate, an associate's degree, or a bachelor's degree. Adequate per-student funding should not be offset by cuts in the total number of students educated. As outlined above, policies that shift students from public community colleges to for-profit institutions are penny wise and pound foolish.

Individual colleges will know best how to invest adequate resources, but some may wish to remedy unequal access to highly qualified full-time faculty (see Figure 7). Many community college faculty members are excellent teachers, but investing in more full-time faculty at community colleges and high-quality professional development for all community college faculties may prove very cost effective. Additional incentives should be created to ensure that the strongest faculty members are connected with the neediest students.

In addition to seeking adequate funding through the legislative process, we encourage equity advocates to begin exploring the possibility of filing lawsuits in those states that have a constitutional guarantee that may extend to higher education. Litigation requiring adequate funding at the K–12 level has been successful in a number of states, and while most state constitutions focus exclusively on elementary and secondary education, a subset of states have language referencing "universities," "schools of higher education," or students up to ages 20 or 21.[80] Lawsuits might have a particularly strong chance of prevailing when aimed at providing adequate funding of developmental education, an important service provided by community colleges, which must bring underprepared students up to speed. Education finance experts note that while it may be difficult to extend adequate funding litigation to noncompulsory higher education in general, the remedial education funding argument may have a greater chance of success because the need of students for remedial college education is a direct result of the failure of the state to provide an adequate education the first time around in high school. Some state constitutions have been read to require career and college readiness, so students who have not received that level of education in high school may deserve to receive it free of charge in a community college setting. In the special education area, students who have not received services they deserved before age 18 have won the right to receive them subsequently.

We emphasize that "adequate" funding does not seek a leveling down of resources in which two-year colleges take from four-year universities. Most of higher education has already suffered damaging cuts in public resources. Instead, we envision a leveling up of investments, in which community colleges can provide the same strong opportunities as students receive in the four-year college sector.

Finally, the task force believes that funding should be tied to student outcomes, where data are available, such as job placements, degrees earned, and transfers to four- year institutions. Interim success points should also be established and rewarded, including emergence from college prep into college level courses, successful completion of gateway courses, completion of certifications for job entry, and transfers prior to graduation. In order to promote equity and avoid incentives for "creaming" the most well prepared students, funding should be tied to distance traveled and progress made—that is to say, with consideration of where students start as well as where they end up. In addition, the number of nontraditional, minority, and low-income students who achieve each of these outcomes should be monitored. Outcomes should be measured by actual cohorts of students, not just by rates, to avoid creating perverse incentives for institutions to shed struggling students. And safeguards should be put in place to avoid grade inflation.

In addition, accountability provisions should incorporate a measure of outcomes in relation to public investment in order to avoid a diversion of resources to colleges—many of which are in the for-profit sector—that educate large numbers of low-income students in a highly expensive fashion and often leave them with few marketable skills and large levels of student debt.

The combination of adequate funding and accountability based on outcomes should help spur important innovation and redesign of community colleges, particularly in the area of developmental education. Exciting and promising redesign is under way in a number of institutions and states.[81] We anticipate that additional redesign will flow from a new funding and accountability system, which will yield greater bang for the community college buck.

Establish Greater Transparency Regarding Public Financial Subsidies to Higher Education. As noted earlier, in sorting through the various public subsidies surrounding higher education, there is a lack of transparency regarding the degree to which institutions of higher education benefit not only from direct public subsidies, but also from public tax expenditures in the form of tax breaks for private donations, the tax exemption of endowment-derived income, and the like. In order to bring greater clarity to all types of public support for higher education, we call on the U.S. Departments of Education and Treasury to issue a report on the extent of public subsidies to various types of institutions—and the accompanying benefit to different socioeconomic populations. The accounting should also include the amount of tax subsidies provided to other nonprofits (including religious institutions) so as not to unfairly single out higher education. The report could include a discussion of the feasibility of requiring that institutions calculate and publicly disclose on an annual basis the degree to which they benefit from both direct public funding and public tax expenditures.

To be clear, the Task Force is not calling for a reduction in incentives for philanthropic giving, but rather a more complete accounting of who gets what in public support. We do not believe higher education funding should be viewed as a zero sum game. Rather, the relatively generous funding of four-year private institutions (and their relatively high success rates) provides reason to believe much more could be accomplished if two-year institutions were adequately funded.

Innovations in Governance to Reduce Economic and Racial Stratification in Higher Education and Strengthen the Ties between Two- and Four-Year Institutions

Our second set of recommendations goes beyond the issue of unequal financing to address the underlying issue of economic and racial stratification itself. As the evidence outlined above suggests, even if we could in theory completely address financial inequities between two- and four-year colleges, there is reason to believe that ignoring the effects of social composition on institutional norms and expectations would miss part of the reason stratification takes a toll.

Economic and racial hierarchies—in which wealthy and white students trend toward selective four-year colleges and working-class and minority students trend toward community colleges—are familiar, but they are in no sense natural or inevitable. They are instead the result of deliberate policy decisions that can be altered for the better.

To date, most of the focus on reducing stratification has involved racial affirmative action programs to integrate elite colleges by race and ethnicity,

---

BOX 2
**Is It Morally Problematic to Encourage More
Middle-Class Students to Attend Community Colleges,
Given the Possibility of Reduced Outcomes?**

Given students' reduced chance of gaining a bachelor's degree when starting at a community college compared with those who begin at four-year institutions, are there moral concerns about encouraging more middle-class students with the resources and preparation to start at four-year institutions to attend two-year colleges instead? We think there are not.

We recommend a number of measures (including adequate funding, strengthening transfer policies, expanding honors colleges, and so on) which we believe will have a positive effect on outcomes for all students—including middle-class students—at community colleges. These steps are both desirable in their own right, and a precondition for integration. The experiences of magnet schools in K–12 settings suggest that efforts to attract middle-class students are unlikely to be successful without simultaneously improving quality. Accordingly, we urge the adoption of a number of quality-enhancing programs, which then should create a virtuous cycle, as the presence of more middle-class students strengthens the political and social capital of two-year institutions, which should improve quality further.

---

but integration should be a two-way street, with efforts to magnetize community colleges as well. In this section, we not only recommend efforts to expand affirmative action programs at four-year institutions to include consideration of socioeconomic status, we also advocate ways for community colleges to educate a broader cross-section of students, including upper-middle class students, in a way that benefits all pupils (See Box 2). By economically integrating community colleges, we can increase the chances of improving two-year institutions themselves—the places where the large bulk of economically disadvantaged students are educated.

Our recommendations below are aimed not only at institutions (which can adopt programs to reduce stratification) but also, importantly, at states and the federal government, which can exercise critical policy levers.

Encourage the Growth of Redesigned Institutions That Strengthen the Connections between Community Colleges and Four-Year Colleges. Among the most promising strategies for reducing stratification—and enhancing student outcomes—is to find ways to connect what are now separate two- and four-year institutional silos. Increasing the ties between institutions could have the effect not only of reducing the economic and racial stratification of the student populations, but also would, by definition, reduce institutional stratification itself. By strengthening connections between two- and four-year institutions, fewer students would be lost in what can often be a difficult process of transfer to four-year settings, in which credits fail to transfer with students and different financial aid policies may exist. By blending elements of two- and four-year colleges in one setting, these institutions may also draw a broader cross section of students than community colleges do.

Richard Atkinson, the former president of the University of California, has noted that these new arrangements can take several forms.[82] Under the "university centers" arrangement, Atkinson and his colleague Saul Geiser note, four-year universities offer upper-division classes at two-year campuses, enabling students to participate who, for reasons of work, family, or residence need to avail themselves of a four-year education in a local community college setting. In this construct, the senior institution awards the actual degree.[83] Under the "branch campuses" model, community colleges are converted into "lower-division satellites of state universities, thereby expanding capacity at the 4-year level and eliminating the need for the traditional transfer process."[84] A third alternative, the community college baccalaureate model, provides state authorization for community colleges to offer bachelor's degrees under certain conditions.

Many of these blended arrangements are nationally recognized as successful. Macomb Community College in Michigan, for example, which enrolls roughly 59,000 students, has partnered with Oakland University and Wayne State University to offer concurrent enrollment in bachelor's programs. Classes for these programs are taught by faculty from participating university partners, but the classes are held at Macomb University Center on Macomb's Center Campus. President Obama chose Macomb as the venue to announce his 2009 American Graduation Initiative.

The state of Florida is particularly known for the ability of two-year community colleges to grant bachelor's degrees in certain areas. In 2008, the Florida legislature renamed the state's community college system as the Florida College System in an effort to increase bachelor's degree production in the state. Under the new Florida College System, a community college may apply to the state to offer bachelor's degrees and become a "State College." All institutions in the system must retain an open door admissions policy, and bachelor's programs must meet criteria for high quality and low cost. Of the twenty-eight institutions in the Florida College System, nineteen currently offer approved bachelor's programs, with most programs in education, business, and nursing.[85]

We applaud these types of efforts but also believe that baccalaureate authority for community colleges should be extended cautiously to avoid negative consequences, such as limiting access and diverting attention from instruction to research. Community college baccalaureate authority should be provided where doing so does not duplicate the programs of nearby four-year institutions, and where it provides new access to place-bound students and addresses unmet labor market demands. Nationwide, twenty-one states now permit community colleges to award baccalaureate degrees.[86] While some have suggested that any granting of such degree authority to community colleges involves "mission creep," diluting the open-access nature of community colleges, Willis N. Holcombe, chancellor of the Florida College system, says that, if done properly, it need not. "The mission has not changed," he says. "Now we are just providing even more access."[87]

There are many reasons that a state may wish to allow community colleges to grant bachelor's degrees. For example, as a practical matter, states that lack the funding capacity to build new four-year colleges are likely to turn to community colleges to produce more baccalaureate degrees. We note here that this sort of arrangement is also beneficial to the extent it reduces disparities between the types of student populations found in two and four-year colleges.[88]

Take Concrete Steps to Facilitate Community College Transfer. Community colleges have, among others, two central functions—serving students whose ultimate goal is a certificate or associate's degree, and serving students who wish to continue on to a bachelor's degree. As noted earlier, certificates can be very valuable in the labor market, and many students who earn certificates may go on to both earn wages and continue their educations. But in recent decades, the transfer function of community colleges has been increasingly eclipsed, as only about one in ten students entering community college earns a bachelor's degree within six years, though eight in ten say they would eventually like to.[89] This development is especially problematic given the way in which the premium associated with a four-year as opposed to a two-year degree has grown considerably over time. U.S. Census data show that the mean earnings of workers age 18 and over with a bachelor's degree has increased relative to that of workers with some college/associate's degree, from 47 percent more in 1975 to 68 percent more in 2010.[90]

Research from the Jack Kent Cooke Foundation finds that talented community college students can transfer and thrive in even the most selective four-year colleges and universities. The foundation's Community College Transfer Initiative, begun in 2005, has allowed community college students to transfer to eight highly selective four-year institutions—Amherst, Bucknell, Cornell, Mount Holyoke, U.C. Berkeley, the University of Michigan at Ann Arbor, the University of North Carolina at Chapel Hill, and the University of Southern California. Preliminary data suggest the transfer students have comparable grade point averages and graduation rates to non-transfer students.[91] Other programs, such as the Edvance Foundation's "Nexpectation Network" are supporting transfers between two-year institutions and private colleges and universities. Research from William Bowen and colleagues, likewise, finds that at public state flagship universities, transfer students are as likely to graduate as those who start at flagships as first years, and community college transfer students have an even greater chance of graduating than first years at less selective four-year institutions.[92]

Accordingly, we recommend these steps to facilitate transfers:

- States should promote stronger articulation and transfer policies. The Western Interstate Commission for Higher Education has identified a number of promising practices that make for effective state transfer policies, including creating a plan for community college students to complete a core of general education courses, establishing clear channels to communicate information about transfer policies to institutions and students, and collecting data to evaluate the policies against set objectives. "Guaranteed transfer" programs can also be a powerful part of state articulation policies. Florida, Nevada, and New Hampshire, for example, all have policies that guarantee admission to a four-year institution for community college students meeting specified requirements.[93] To cite two illustrations, Valencia College, in Florida, winner of the 2011 Aspen Prize for Community College Excellence, has an agreement with the University of Central Florida called "DirectConnect." Under the policy, "students cannot transfer to UCF without an associate's degree, but cannot be denied admission if they have one from Valencia." (Valencia is also an example of the "university centers" arrangement, as UCF has an outpost at Valencia.)[94] To take another example, Miami Dade College has a similar relationship with Florida International University. About half of Florida International students arrive from Miami Dade.

- States and/or the federal government should offer financial incentives to four-year colleges that accept economically disadvantaged community college transfer students.
- Four-year institutions should provide a clear, predictable pathway for students to transfer from community college. For example, Syracuse University seeks to provide community college students with a predicted financial aid package if they transfer to Syracuse.
- Task Force member Gail Mellow has suggested that Ivy League institutions commit "to accepting transfer students from community colleges for 1% of their junior class." If this step were taken, "privileged students would begin to encounter students from the other 99%," and transfer students "would provide living proof that intelligence, drive, and achievement are not the sole province of students born to good fortune."[95] We would like to take this excellent idea even further and call on all highly selective four-year colleges and universities to commit to accepting community college transfers for 5 percent of their junior class. This 5 percent proposal seems eminently reasonable given that some elite institutions, such as the University of California at Berkeley and at Los Angeles—where roughly one-third of new students enrolling in 2008–09 were transfers from California community colleges—have already surpassed this goal.[96]
- On the community college side, we think two-year institutions that do an unusually effective job of promoting transfer to four-year colleges (in light of their demographic mix) should be celebrated in an alternative to traditional school rankings that do not consider socioeconomic and racial characteristics of institutions.

Strengthening transfer policies not only would benefit those students who transfer, but also could draw a broader economic mix to community colleges, strengthening the political and social capital of two-year institutions. To the extent that community colleges are today viewed by middle-class families as institutions in which few students ultimately go on to earn a four-year degree, community colleges will remain unattractive to such families. Conversely, strong transfer programs from two- to four-year colleges should entice more students to begin at affordable two-year institutions before moving on to receive a bachelor's degree. At a time when many American families are concerned about affording college for their children, a strengthened community college transfer process could substantially reduce the overall cost of a four-year degree.

In addition, more should be done to ensure that student credit hours—from two- or four-year institutions—are recognized in the form of a degree or certificate. According to the Georgetown Center for Education and the Workforce, 36 million Americans (more than 20 percent of the working adult population) have enrolled in college but have not completed a degree; and some one-third of this group (12–17 million) have completed more than sixty credit hours but received no recognition of their learning in the form of a degree or credential like an associate degree.[97] We believe that state education systems should explore and scale-up consistent approaches to awarding associate degrees to students who transfer from community colleges to universities, in order to fairly credit community colleges for their work in preparing transfer students and help individuals by providing them a postsecondary credential with proven currency in the labor market.

Innovation in Racially and Economically Inclusive Community College Honors Programs. Honors programs are an important "magnet" feature of community colleges, a way of reducing both racial and economic stratification. These programs, which are found on more than 160 community college campuses, range from those that offer entirely separate programs and have strict enrollment criteria to those that offer supplementary honors seminars to students above a certain grade point average and also provide advice on the transition to four-year colleges.[98]

If one objective of having an honors program is to draw talented students from a range of economic and racial backgrounds, the challenge is to simultaneously offer programs that will be highly attractive to students who might not otherwise consider community college and yet at the same time avoid becoming tracking devices that segregate students within community colleges. Two distinct approaches may enable community college honors programs to thread this needle.

One possibility is to make honors programs accessible to a wide range of students by employing flexible requirements. A promising example is the honors program in Highline Community College in Des Moines, Washington, which does not have separate courses for honors students but rather pushes students to complete extra projects and papers in classes that are accessible to all. Students self-elect to join the honors program, and anyone with a 3.5 GPA and twelve credit hours is eligible. Furthermore, students may participate in the honors program at varying levels: students who fulfill all the course requirements of the honors program graduate as Honors Scholars, but those who fall short of this mark may still earn honors credit for individual courses. In addition, all honors students, even those who do not graduate as Honors Scholars, benefit from the personal advising, interdisciplinary academic work, and priority registration afforded to participants of the program.[99] Although Highline does not offer socioeconomic data for their honors program, they do provide information about the cultural and racial makeup which suggests that enrollment is quite diverse. More than 40 percent of Honors Scholars are nonwhite, and one-third are male.[100] Less than half of the students in the honors program are "born-in-the-U.S. Caucasians."[101]

A second model is the Honors College at Miami Dade College, which has stricter enrollment criteria than the program at Highline and a less fluid structure. At Miami Dade, students must meet a certain threshold for high school GPA, SAT, or ACT; submit an essay and recommendations; and participate in an interview.[102] The Honors College at Miami Dade is more distinct from the rest of the institution than is the Highline honors program. Of the sixty credits needed to earn an associate's degree, Honors College students have to take at least thirty-six credits in honors courses, which typically enroll only Honors College students. (Students outside the Honors College may get special permission to enroll in certain Honors College courses.) When the Honors College was created, Miami Dade ran ads in the community and gave Honors College faculty special training that included familiarizing them with "the honors mystique."[103]

An honors program structured like Miami Dade's, with a competitive admissions process and largely separate programming, could be susceptible to tracking more affluent students. It has not been the case at Miami Dade, and community colleges can avoid tracking by taking affirmative steps to consider socioeconomic disadvantage in admissions and recruiting applicants from across the student body.

We recommend dedicated state and federal funding programs—akin to the federal Magnet Schools Assistance Program in K–12 schooling — to encourage community colleges to adopt honors programs under the condition that these programs (1) are sufficiently large in size to make a difference in the social composition of the campus as a whole; and (2) are inclusive and do not become privileged enclaves and separate tracks within institutions.

Encourage Innovation in Early College Programs that Enhance Community College Diversity. "Early college" programs, some of which allow talented high school students to take advanced courses at community colleges,[104] may provide a way of attracting high-achieving and middle-class populations to community colleges that are racially and economically isolated.

Most "dual credit" classes, which allow high school students to simultaneously earn college credit, are offered on high school campuses, but 23 percent are taught on a postsecondary campus, often a community college.[105] Because dual credit classes often attract academically advanced students who are sometimes charged tuition for courses, some research suggests students enrolled in dual credit classes may be more affluent than the general public school population.[106]

At the same time, if properly structured, early college classes on community college campuses could provide an opportunity to create socioeconomically diverse settings because programs rarely offer separate classes for high school and college students. According to U.S. Department of Education data, of schools that offered academic dual credit classes on a postsecondary campus, 82 percent enrolled both high school and postsecondary students in the classes.[107] Of schools that offered career/technical dual credit classes on a postsecondary campus, 78 percent enrolled both high school and postsecondary students in the classes.[108]

We recommend federal funding of those early college programs that would have the effect of better integrating two-year institutions that are racially and economically isolated. We also recommend that financial incentives be put in place to offset the cost of early college programs to community colleges. (Community colleges now bear the bulk of costs, as high school students are ineligible for federal financial aid.)

Prioritize Funding of New Programs for Economically and Racially Isolated Community Colleges. In addition to addressing stratification between the community college and four-year college sectors, there is the additional issue of socioeconomic and racial stratification between individual two-year institutions. As noted above, background research for this Task Force conducted by Sara Goldrick-Rab and Peter Kinsley finds that "more than three-quarters of the variation in racial composition among community colleges is directly attributable to the racial composition of their surrounding geographic locales." But the study also finds that 10 percent of institutions "enroll a less-segregated student body than geography alone would predict."[109]

Because many low-income community college students have little choice in where they will attend college, we recommend that state and federal funding programs for honors programs, early college, and other initiatives be directed first to those community colleges with few middle-class students, just as attractive magnet programs are placed in higher poverty elementary and secondary schools

Policymakers should also be cognizant of economic and racial disparities within individual community colleges between different degree programs.

Provide Incentives for Four-Year Institutions to Engage in Affirmative Action for Low-Income Students of All Races to Match Community College Diversity Efforts. A better designed system of higher education requires that four-year institutions do more to educate low-income and minority students. To the extent that community colleges are able to create magnet-type programs to attract more middle-class students, this development could exacerbate overcrowding problems. Accordingly, the movement of students should flow in both directions, so that middle-class students move into community colleges and low-income students who might have gone to community college are given access to four-year colleges.

There is a great deal of evidence that four-year institutions could do a much better job of attracting "strivers," low-income students who achieve at higher levels than expected given the disadvantages they face. Research finds that while colleges do take affirmative steps to increase racial and ethnic diversity, most do virtually nothing to increase socioeconomic diversity.[110] There is also a great deal of evidence that many low-income students could perform well, even in the most selective institutions. Anthony P. Carnevale and Stephen J. Rose found that the most selective 146 institutions could boost the proportion of students who come from the bottom half of the socioeconomic distribution from the current share of 10 percent to 38 percent, and graduation rates would remain as high as they are today.[111] Likewise, new research from Stanford's Caroline Hoxby and Harvard's Christopher Avery finds that a substantial portion of high-scoring, low-income students do not attend selective colleges and are ripe for recruitment.[112]

The effort to recruit promising low-income students to four-year institutions is important in its own right. It will provide new opportunities for low-income students and the greater diversity created will benefit the education of all students. But expanded efforts would also serve as a complement to plans enacted by community colleges to attract more middle-class students by relieving overcrowding at the community college level. In short, breaking down stratification between two- and four-year colleges will require deliberate programs on the part of both sets of institutions.

Indeed, we recommend that every state policy, federal policy, or institutional practice that aims to increase diversity in community colleges should be matched by a state policy, federal policy, or institutional practice that aims to increase diversity on four-year campuses. Thus, if states create bachelor's degree programs at community colleges, thereby attracting more affluent students to those institutions, an equal amount of funding and effort should be allocated to ensuring that low-income students attend four-year colleges through, for example, increases in need-based aid and improved high school guidance efforts. If honors programs result in more white students attending community colleges, equal efforts should be made to ensure that four-year colleges enroll and graduate larger shares of minority students. (See Box 3.)

To provide teeth to this policy, we recommend that the diversity of students at every level of higher education—two-year and four-year—in each state be monitored regularly to assess whether access and success for different student populations by race and income is being at least maintained, if not increased, as a result of new community college diversification policies. If the net effect is lower rates of higher education access and completion for low-income and minority populations, those policies should be reversed.

The earlier recommendation to provide institutions with "adequacy-based" funding (with a premium for low-income students with greater needs) should itself provide some financial incentive for four-year institutions to recruit disadvantaged students more aggressively. In addition, to spur further movement in favor of socioeconomic diversity at four-year institutions, we recommend that influential college rankings be modified to consider socioeconomic diversity as a measure of quality. Socioeconomic diversity could be enhanced either by initially recruiting and admitting more low-income students, or by accepting larger numbers of low-income community college transfers.

To provide additional incentives for four-year colleges to enroll and graduate low-income students, we recommend the creation of a cash prize for the four-year college that increases Pell enrollment and graduation the most. On the flip side, we recommend the prominent publication by the U.S. Department of Education of a "worst offenders" list of the least economically diverse four-year schools in the country.

BOX 3
Concerns about Displacement

Any attempt to reduce stratification by attracting more middle-class students to community colleges raises the specter that low-income students might be displaced, a very grave concern for members of the task force as this would undercut the central mission of two-year institutions: to expand access and serve students not well-served by the larger system of higher education. Many states, particularly California, have seen drastic budget cuts, which have resulted in the elimination of course offerings, often to the detriment of low-income students, who may have less access to knowledge about ways to work the system when course slots are limited.

We believe serious concerns about displacement can be addressed if the key recommendations are implemented in tandem. First, the two-way strategy—economic affirmative action at four year institutions implemented in conjunction with enhanced "magnet" offerings at community colleges—should alleviate space constraints at either institution. If active steps are taken to counsel more qualified low-income and minority students to attend four-year colleges, spaces at two-year institutions will open up. Second, the new adequacy-based funding proposals—backed up by litigation—should enhance the financial position of community colleges, providing the resources to address any needs for expansion. In the long run, moreover, the greater presence of middle-class students should enhance the responsiveness of the political system to the need to provide sufficient funding to community colleges. To ensure no low-income and working-class community college students are displaced, our recommendations include a requirement that four-year diversity efforts must precisely match two-year diversity efforts.

Ultimately, the special mission of community colleges is not only to serve low-income and working class students, but to serve them well. Drawing upon a greater cross-section of American college students should enable community colleges to accomplish that goal—with greater resources, and enhanced expectations—far better than our current highly stratified system has.

CONCLUSION

Taken together, we believe these innovations in financing and governance of higher education—though not the only solutions—can dramatically enhance the prospect of millions of students attending our nation's community colleges. The two primary strategies outlined—adequacy-based funding and de-stratification of student populations—go hand in glove.

Efforts to make inadequacies in community college funding more transparent, coupled with legal efforts to address underfunding, should make it possible to improve the quality of community colleges. Improved quality, in turn, may attract a broader cross-section of students, including those from more affluent backgrounds. The de-stratification that flows from increased quality, coupled with deliberate efforts to de-stratify higher education, should further promote the virtuous cycle. Less stratification should help create political capital to sustain investments in community colleges; and the higher expectations of less-stratified community college populations should help create "transfer cultures" that will improve outcomes for low-income students beyond the benefits associated merely with greater financial resources.

We recognize that in times of tight budgets, many policymakers see higher education as a target for cuts. But a wide body of research suggests that if we want to have a more prosperous nation, we need to supply businesses with well-trained personnel.[113] This will require long-term investments and critical changes to our system of college and universities.

Our nation is experiencing profound demographic change. In May 2012, the U.S. Census Bureau released estimates showing that, for the first time, a majority (50.4 percent) of Americans less than a year old are racial or ethnic minorities.[114] The U.S. Census Bureau projects that the percentage of the population ages 0–19 that is non-Hispanic white alone will drop from its 2010 level of 55.5 percent to 48.8 percent in 2025, and down to 38.1 percent in 2050.[115] Our entire society has an enormous stake in ensuring that we tap into the talents of all of our children.

Today, community colleges are in great danger of becoming indelibly separate and unequal institutions in the higher education landscape. As *Brown v. Board of Education* helped galvanize our nation to address deep and enduring inequalities that had long been taken for granted, so today it is time to address—head on—abiding racial and economic inequalities in our system of American higher education. While we believe in sharing best practices, we believe that discussion is overly narrow. It is time to take bold action to enhance the role of community colleges in strengthening American competitiveness, bolstering American democracy, and reviving the American Dream.

APPENDIX:
LIMITATIONS OF THE INTEGRATED POSTSECONDARY EDUCATION DATA SYSTEM (IPEDS) ON EVALUATING GRADUATION RATES OF COMMUNITY COLLEGE STUDENTS

The College Board has concluded that "a major limitation of [the IPEDS institutional graduation rate] is that it only counts full-time, first-time students who begin in the fall, but most community college students initially enroll part time (often due to family or work responsibilities) and are not included."[116] The College Board then cites a 2009 article written by the Institute for Higher Education Leadership & Policy (IHELP), at Sacramento State's Jeremy Offenstein and Nancy Shulock, who identify five major problems with IPEDS graduation rates:

1. "Unclear student goals complicate the assessment of meaningful outcomes for students." Community college students attend for a variety of reasons, making it difficult to identify which students are really "degree-seeking." In addition, "students may indicate that they are degree-seeking for the purpose of getting financial aid even though they do not intend to earn a degree."

2. "Many students are excluded." "Graduation and transfer-out rates only include students who attend full time and begin in the summer or fall term. This restriction was intended to level the playing field across colleges since some colleges serve much higher proportions of part-time, low-income students. Limiting graduation and transfer-out rates to 'like' students across colleges was felt to lead to more meaningful comparisons. But this choice has made graduation rate data virtually meaningless because fewer than half of community college students fit these criteria. In fact, national data suggest that only 39% of first-time, public two-year students attended full time, initially enrolled in the fall or summer, and planned on earning a degree or certificate. In contrast, 43% of beginning public two-year students planned on earning a degree or certificate but either did not attend full time during their first term of enrollment or enrolled at a time other than the summer or fall. The restrictions based on attendance and initial term of enrollment disproportionately exclude certain groups of students. In particular, the graduation and transfer-out rates tend to exclude adult students who are more likely to attend part time."

3. "Time allowed for completion is unrealistic and problematic for certificates." Even rates calculated using 200 percent of normal time may be too short considering the fact that so many community college students attend part-time at some point.
4. "Student mobility complicates tracking completion and identifying first-time students."
5. "The concept of 'transfer' in IPEDS is flawed." On one hand, the measure undercounts the total number of students who transfer from community colleges to four-year institutions. Students who complete degree programs at community colleges before transferring to four-year institutions and students who fail to notify the community college of their transfer are not counted. On the other hand, the measure also includes lateral transfers, when a student transfers from one community college to another community college.[117]

NOTES

1. Christopher M. Mullin, "Why Access Matters: The Community College Student Body," American Association of Community Colleges Policy Brief 2012-01PBL, February 2012, 4.

2. U.S. Department of Education, National Center for Education Statistics, Integrated Postsecondary Education Data System (IPEDS), http://nces.ed.gov/ipeds/datacenter/. These figures are for twelve-month enrollment at degree-granting institutions in the United States, 2010–11. The percentage of undergraduate students served by community colleges is smaller if fall enrollment or all institutions (including non-degree-granting) are selected.

3. Among all 2003–04 first-time postsecondary students, 49.4 percent earned a certificate, associate's degree, or bachelor's degree within six years; 50.6 percent of students had not earned a degree or certificate within six years (15 percent of students were still enrolled after six years, while 35.5 percent were no longer enrolled). "Six-Year Attainment, Persistence, Transfer, Retention, and Withdrawal Rates of Students Who Began Postsecondary Education in 2003–04," U.S. Department of Education, July 2011, Table 2.0-A, 17, http://nces.ed.gov/pubs2011/2011152.pdf. After six years, then, the college dropout rate is 36 percent and many of the remaining 15 percent of students still enrolled may never complete, as the likelihood of completion declines with time. The nonprofit National Student Clearinghouse Research Center offer somewhat more favorable data than the federal government. The Clearinghouse recently reported a 54 percent six-year graduation rate among first-time students. See National Student Clearinghouse Research Center, *Signature Report: Completing College: A National View of Student Attainment Rates,* November 2012, 6. By contrast, the overall high school dropout rate among the population ages 16 to 24 in 2010 was 7.4 percent; "Table 116: Percentage of High School Dropouts among Persons 16 through 24 Years Old (Status Dropout Rate), by Sex and Race/Ethnicity: Selected Years, 1960 through 2010," *Digest of Education Statistics,* U.S. Department of Education, National Center for Education Statistics, 2011, http://nces.ed.gov/programs/digest/d11/tables/dt11_116.asp.

4. Claudia Golden and Lawrence F. Katz, *The Race between Education and Technology* (Cambridge, Mass.: Harvard University Press, 2008), 1.

5. "United States," in *Education at a Glance 2012: OECE Indicators* (Paris: OECD, 2012), http://dx.doi.org/10.1787/eag-2012-en. These data do not include certificates.

6. Excerpts of the President's remarks in Warren, Michigan, White House, Office of the Press Secretary, July 14, 2009, http://www.whitehouse.gov/the_press_office/Excerpts-of-the-Presidents-remarks-in-Warren-Michigan-and-fact-sheet-on-the-American-Graduation-Initiative/ (accessed March 1, 2011); Thomas Bailey, "Can Community Colleges Achieve Ambitious Graduation Goals?" draft, prepared for the American Enterprise Institute Conference, *Degrees of Difficulty: Can American Higher Education Regain Its Edge?* February 15, 2011, 5, www.aei.org/event/100346.

7. Bailey, "Can Community Colleges Achieve Ambitious Graduation Goals?" 15.

8. Laura Horn and Paul Skomsvold, *Community College Student Outcomes: 1994–2009* (Washington, D.C.: U.S. Department of Education, Institute of Education Sciences, and National Center for Education Statistics, November 2011), Tables 1-A, 5-A and 7-A., http://nces.ed.gov/pubs2012/2012253.pdf.

9. "Reclaiming the American Dream: Community Colleges at the Nation's Future," A Report From the 21st-Century Commission on the Future of Community Colleges, 2012, viii.

10. Donna M. Desrochers and Jane V. Wellman, *Trends in College Spending: 1999–2009: Where Does the Money Come From? Where Does It Go? What Does It Buy?* (Washington, D.C.: Delta Cost Project, 2011), 7, 13, and 23, http://www.deltacostproject.org/resources/pdf/Trends2011_Final_090711.pdf.

11. Some community college programs (for example, nursing), do have entrance requirements.

12. Douglas N. Harris, "Ending the Blame Game on Educational Inequity: A Study of 'High Flying' Schools and NCLB," Educational Policy Studies Laboratory, Arizona State University, March 2006, 20.

13. U.S. Department of Education, Institute of Educational Sciences, National Center for Education Statistics, National Assessments of Educational Progress (NAEP), 2011 Math Assessment, Grade 4.

14. Heather Schwartz, *Housing Policy Is School Policy: Economically Integrative Housing Promotes Academic Success in Montgomery County, Maryland* (New York: Century Foundation, 2010), 24, Figure 6.

15. Marco Basile, "The Cost Effectiveness of Socioeconomic School Integration," in *The Future of School Integration: Socioeconomic Diversity as an Education Reform Strategy*, ed. Richard D. Kahlenberg (New York: The Century Foundation Press, 2012), 141–44.

16. See Kahlenberg, *The Future of School Integration*, 309–11.

17. See Genevieve Siegel-Hawley and Erica Frankenberg, "Magnet School Student Outcomes: What the Research Says," National Coalition for School Diversity, Research Brief #6, http://prrac.org/pdf/DiversityResearchBriefNo6.pdf; and Jennifer Jellison Holme and Amy Stuart Wells, "School Choice beyond District Borders: Lessons for the Reauthorization of NCLB from Interdistrict Desegregation and Open Enrollment Plans," in *Improving on No Child Left Behind: Getting Education Reform Back on Track*, ed. Richard D. Kahlenberg (New York: The Century Foundation Press, 2008).

18. Greg J. Duncan and Richard J. Murnane, "Introduction: The American Dream, Then and Now," in *Whither Opportunity? Rising Inequality, Schools, and Children's Life Chances*, ed. Greg J. Duncan and Richard J. Murnane (New York: Russell Sage Foundation and Spencer Foundation, 2011), 11.

19. Bruce Baker, Lori Taylor, and Arnold Vedlitz, "Adequacy Estimates and the Implications of Common Standards for the Cost of Instruction," Report to the National Research Council, May 30, 2008, 14, Table 2, http://www.educationjustice.

org/assets/files/pdf/Resources/Policy/Funding%20Systems/Adequacy%20estimates%20and%20the%20implications%20of%20common%20standards%20for%20the%20cost%20of%20instruction.pdf.

20. Bruce D. Baker, "Evaluating the Reliability, Validity and Usefulness of Education Cost Studies," *Journal of Education Finance* 32, no. 2 (2006): 170–201, cited in Bruce D. Baker and Preston C. Green, "Politics, Empirical Evidence, and Policy Design: The Case of School Finance and the Costs of Educational Adequacy" in *Handbook of Education Politics and Policy*, ed. Bruce S. Cooper, James G. Cibulka, and Lance D. Fusarelli (New York: Routledge, 2008), 318.

21. Deborah A. Verstegen and Teresa S. Jordan, "A Fifty-State Survey of School Finance Policies and Programs: An Overview," *Journal of Education Finance* 34, no. 3 (Winter 2009): 221.

22. See e.g. Anthony Carnevale and Stephen Rose, "Socioeconomic Status, Race/Ethnicity, and Selective College Admissions," in *America's Untapped Resource: Low-Income Students in Higher Education*, ed. Richard D. Kahlenberg (New York: The Century Foundation Press, 2004), 135.

23. U.S. Census Bureau, *School Enrollment, Educational Attainment, and Illiteracy: October 1952*, "Table 11. Years of School Completed by Civilian Noninstitutional Population 14 Years Old and Over, by Age and Sex, for the United States: October 1952," 18, http://www.census.gov/hhes/socdemo/education/data/cps/1952/tab-11.pdf.

24. Josipa Roksa, Eric Grodsky, Richard Arum and Adam Gamoran, "United States: Changes in Higher Education and Social Stratification," in Yossi Shavit, Richard Arum, and Adam Gamoran, *Stratification in Higher Education: A Comparative Study* (Stanford, Calif.: Stanford University Press, 2007), 166.

25. Anthony Carnevale and Jeff Strohl, "How Increasing College Access Is Increasing Inequality, and What to Do About It," in *Rewarding Strivers: Helping Low-Income Students Succeed in College*, ed. Richard D. Kahlenberg (New York: The Century Foundation Press, 2010).

26. U.S. Census Bureau, *Educational Attainment in the United States: 2011—Detailed Tables*, "Table 3. Detailed Years of School Completed by People 25 Years and Over by Sex, Age Groups, Race and Hispanic Origin: 2011," http://www.census.gov/hhes/socdemo/education/data/cps/2011/tables.html.

27. Carnevale and Strohl, "How Increasing College Access is Increasing Inequality, and What to Do About It," 131–32. Roughly one-quarter of degree-seeking community college students come from immigrant backgrounds. Robert T. Teranishi, Carola Suárez-Orozco, and Marcelo Suárez-Orozco, "Immigrants in Community Colleges," *The Future of Children* 21, no. 1 (Spring 2011): 155, http://icy.gseis.ucla.edu/articles/immigrants-in-community-colleges/.

28. In 2010, 33 percent of students in two-year public colleges were black and Latino compared with just 20 percent of students at private nonprofit four-year institutions. *Digest of Education Statistics* 2011, Table 241, cited in Baum and Kurose, 76, Table 1.

29. Goldrick-Rab and Kinsley, 121, Table 2.

30. Carnevale and Strohl, "How Increasing College Access Is Increasing Inequality," 136–37. See also Baum and Kurose, 77, Figure 1 (citing federal data suggesting in 2007–08, the highest income quartile representation at community colleges had dropped to 15 percent).

31. Carnevale and Strohl, "How Increasing College Access Is Increasing Inequality," 131–32.

32. See "How America Pays for College 2011: Sallie Mae's National Study of College Students and Parents, Summary Report," conducted by Ipsos Public Affairs (2011), 12, https://www.salliemae.com/assets/Core/how-America-pays/HowAmerica PaysforCollege_2011.pdf (finding that the share of low-income students attending two-year public colleges as opposed to other colleges increased from 20 percent in academic year 2007–08 to 33 percent in academic year 2010–11, while the share of middle-income students increased from 27 percent to 29 percent and the share of high income students from 16 percent to 22 percent. Between 2007–08 and 2010–11, the share of low-income students attending two-year public institutions increased by thirteen percentage points, middle-income by two percentage points, and high income by six percentage points; expressed in terms of percentage increases, the share of low-income students attending two-year public institutions increased by 65 percent, middle-income by 7 percent, and high-income by 25 percent).

33. William G. Bowen, Matthew M. Chingos, and Michael S. McPherson, *Crossing the Finish Line: Completing College at America's Public Universities* (Princeton, N.J.: Princeton University Press, 2009), 233.

34. Jennifer Gonzalez, "Education for All?" *Chronicle of Higher Education,* April 22, 2012, citing the Community College Research Center at Columbia University's Teachers College.

35. Desrochers and Wellman, *Trends in College Spending 1999–2009,* 52–57, Figure A2.

36. Baum and Kurose, 87, Table 5. Net tuition revenue at two-year public colleges rose from 18 percent of revenues in 1989 to 27 percent in 2009, as state and local appropriations declined from 72 percent of revenue to 58 percent.

37. Economist Richard Vedder of Ohio University illustrates the point by comparing the public subsidies of a private institution, Princeton University, and a public institution located twelve miles away, the College of New Jersey. On the surface, the College of New Jersey appears more heavily subsidized in the form of state and federal funding of about $2,000 per pupil. But counting foregone tax revenue from endowment income and capital gains (an estimated $245 million in 2010), tax-induced gifts ($100 million), and government grants covering research overhead ($75 million), Vedder estimates the public subsidy of Princeton to be $54,000 per student. By comparison, he estimates the federal tax and research subsidies at the College of New Jersey to be less than $600 per student. Richard Vedder, "Princeton Reaps Tax Breaks as State Colleges Beg," Bloomberg News, March 18, 2012.

38. Jane G. Gravelle, "Tax Issues and University Endowments," Memorandum to Honorable Max Baucus, Chairman, Senate Committee on Finance and Honorable

Chuck Grassley, Ranking Member, Senate Committee on Finance, Congressional Research Service, August 20, 2007; Joint Committee on Taxation, *Estimates of Federal Tax Expenditures for Fiscal Years 2007–2011*, JCS-3-07 (Washington D.C.: Government Printing Office, 2007); and Baum and Kurose, 92–94.

39. Desrochers and Wellman, *Trends in College Spending*, Figure A1, 48–51.

40. Stephen Burd, "Moving on Up: How Tuition Tax Breaks Increasingly Favor the Upper-Middle Class," *Education Sector*, April 19, 2012, available at http://www.educationsector.org/sites/default/files/publications/TaxCredit_CYCT_RELEASED.pdf.

41. Sara Goldrick-Rab, Douglas N. Harris, Christopher Mazzeo, and Gregory Kienzl, "Transforming America's Community Colleges: A Federal Policy Proposal to Expand Opportunity and Promote Economic Prosperity," Brookings Policy Brief, May 2009, 3.

42. Ibid., 5.

43. Tamar Lewin, "Money Urged for Colleges to Perform Job Training," *New York Times*, February 13, 2012, http://www.nytimes.com/2012/02/14/education/obama-to-propose-community-college-aid.html.

44. Bowen et al., *Crossing the Finish Line*, 233.

45. Richard Arum and Josipa Roksa, *Academically Adrift: Limited Learning on College Campuses* (Chicago, Ill.: University of Chicago Press, 2011), 52.

46. Bank, Barbara J., Ricky L. Slavings, and Bruce J. Biddle, "Effects of Peer, Faculty, and Parental Influences on Students' Persistence," *Sociology of Education* 63 (1990): 208–25. For the classic study highlighting the power of peer effects, see Alexander W. Astin, *What Matters in College? Four Critical Years Revisited* (San Francisco: Jossey-Bass Publishers, 1993). Astin, director of the Higher Education Research Institute at UCLA, analyzed more than 140 entering student characteristics and 190 environmental characteristics for almost 25,000 students at four-year institutions and concluded that "the single most important environmental influence on student development is the peer group" (xiv and 398). Moreover, among 35 measures of peer group characteristics, Astin concluded that "peer group SES [socioeconomic status] produced twenty-one significant direct effects on student outcomes, more than any peer group or faculty measure"—including positive cognitive effects on test scores and critical thinking skills (352–53 and 408).

47. Juan Carlos Calcagno, Thomas Bailey, Davis Jenkins, Gregory Kienzl, and Timothy Leinbach, "Community College Student Success: What Institutional Characteristics Make a Difference?" *Economics of Education Review* 27 (2008): 632–45, 636.

48. Steven Brint and Jerome Karabel, *The Diverted Dream: Community Colleges and the Promise of Educational Opportunity in America, 1900–1985* (New York: Oxford University Press, 1989), 119–20. More recent research finds that while a focus on community college associates degrees in vocational fields does not decrease transfer, institutions focusing on vocational short-term certificates do reduce ultimate educational attainment. Josipa Roksa, "Does the Vocational Focus of Community Colleges Hinder Students' Educational Attainment?" *Review of Higher Education* 29, no. 4 (2006): 499–526, 519–20.

49. See e.g. Mariana Alfonso, Thomas R. Bailey, and Marc Scott, "The Educational Outcomes of Occupational Sub-baccalaureate Students: Evidence from the 1990s," *Economics of Education Review* 24, no. 2 (2005): 201–02.

50. Clive R. Belfield and Thomas Bailey, "The Benefits of Attending Community College: A Review of the Evidence," *Community College Review* 39, no. 1 (2011): 53. See also Mina Dadgar and Madeline Joy Weiss, "Labor Market Returns to Sub-Baccalaureate Credentials: How Much Does a Community College Degree or Certificate Pay?" CCRC Working Paper No. 45, Community College Research Center, Teachers College, Columbia University, June 2012, http://ccrc.tc.columbia.edu/Publication.asp?UID=1101, p. 34; and Brian Bosworth, "Certificates Count: An Analysis of Sub-baccalaureate Certificates, Complete College America and Future Works," 2010, p. ii–iii, http://www.complete college.org/docs/Certificates%20Count%20FINAL%2012-05.pdf.

51. Geiser and Atkinson, "Beyond the Master Plan," 8, citing Kevin Dougherty, *The Contradictory College: The Conflict Origins, Impacts, and Futures of the Community College* (Albany: State University of New York Press, 1994).

52. Bailey, "Can Community Colleges Achieve Ambitious Graduation Goals?" 15.

53. U.S. Department of Education, National Center for Education Statistics, *The Digest of Education Statistics 2011*, 2011, Table 345, http://nces.ed.gov/programs/ digest/d11/tables/dt11_345.asp. Data are for the cohort of college students first enrolling in the 2003-04 academic year.

54. Kati Haycock, "Community Colleges Are Not a Silver Bullet for Closing Completion Gap," *Higher Ed Watch*, April 7, 2010.

55. C. Lockwood Reynolds, "Where to Attend? Estimates of the Effects of Beginning a Two-Year College," mimeo, University of Michigan, Ann Arbor, October 25, 2006, cited in Bowen et al., *Crossing the Finish Line*, 134.

56. Bowen et al., *Crossing the Finish Line,* 137–39.

57. Bridget Terry Long and Michal Kurlaender, "Do Community Colleges Provide a Viable Pathway to a Baccalaureate Degree?" NBER Working Paper 14367, September 2008, 26.

58. Anthony Carnevale and Stephen J. Rose, "Engine of Social Mobility and Growth: Refuting Three Myths About Community Colleges," Forthcoming paper, Georgetown University Center for Education and the Workforce, 2013.

59. Bowen et al, *Crossing the Finish Line,* 107–08.

60. Mary Martinez-Wenzl and Rigoberto Marquez, "Unrealized Promises: Unequal Access, Affordability, and Excellence at Community Colleges in Southern California," Civil Rights Project at UCLA, January 2012, 36.

61. Melguizo and Kosiewicz, 139.

62. Ibid., 142–43.

63. Ibid., 144, 143.

64. Ibid., 145, 150.

65. Ibid., 150–152.

66. Ibid., 146.

67. Ibid., 152.

68. Goldrick-Rab and Kinsley, 120–21, Table 2.

69. Ibid.

70. Calcagno, Bailey, Jenkins, Kienzl, and Leinbach, "Community College Student Success" 644. (Instructional expenditure in this study did not have a statistically significant effect.)

71. Goldrick-Rab and Kinsley, 111.

72. Desroachers and Wellman, "Trends," 40, Figure 19. See also Jane Wellman, "Financial Characteristics of Broad Access Public Institutions," Background paper prepared for the Stanford Conference on Mapping Broad Access Higher Education, December 1–2, 2011, 18.

73. Mark Schneider, "The Hidden Costs of Community Colleges," American Enterprise Institute, October, 2011, 2; and Wellman, "Financial Characteristics," 19.

74. Calcagno, Bailey, et al., "Community College Student Success," 644. See also Wellman, "Financial Characteristics of Broad Access Institutions," 21–22, citing three research studies.

75. Baum and Kurose, 87.

76. Calcagno, Bailey, et al. find in their study of NELS data (at 644) that "expanding academic support services seem[s] to benefit the traditional-age student population."

77. Committee on Health, Education, Labor, and Pensions, United States Senate, *For Profit Higher Education: The Failure to Safeguard the Federal Investment and Ensure Student Success* (Washington, D.C.: U.S. Government Printing Office, July 30, 2012), 90–91, http://www.gpo.gov/fdsys/browse/committeecong.action?collection= CPRT&committee=health&chamber=senate&congressplus=112&ycord=0. The investigation found that for-profits charge much more in tuition than community colleges yet higher fees do not translate into higher levels of support for students. The report found that associate's degree programs at for-profits cost an average of four times as much as associate's programs at community colleges. (*For Profit Higher Education*, 4.) And yet resources are much more likely to be devoted to recruiters than support staff. "In 2010," the report concludes, "the for-profit colleges examined employed 35,202 recruiters compared with 3,512 career services staff and 12,452 support services staff, more than two and a half recruiters for each support services employee." (*For Profit Higher Education*, 2.) Although for-profit two-year colleges do not receive the direct public subsidies provided to public community colleges, taxpayers end up paying an enormous amount in financial aid for which the public receives little in return. In 2009–10, the Senate committee study concluded, for-profit colleges received $32 billion, 25 percent of the total Department of Education student aid program funds, despite the fact that students at for-profit colleges make up just 9.1 percent of all students at degree-granting institutions. U.S. Department of Education, National Center for Education Statistics, *Digest of Education Statistics 2011*, Table 196, "Enrollment, staff, and degrees/certificates conferred in postsecondary institutions participating in Title IV programs, by level and control of institution, sex of student, type of staff, and type of degree: Fall 2009 and 2009–10," http://nces.ed.gov/programs/digest/d11/tables/dt11_196.asp. See also *For Profit*

Colleges, 3. Moreover, the researchers found: "Students who attended a for-profit college accounted for 47 percent of all Federal student loan defaults." (*For Profit Colleges,* 9.) Accordingly, the under-funding of community colleges, which pushes increasing number of students into for-profit institutions, is highly inefficient.

78. See American Association of Colleges and Universities, "High Impact Educational Practices," http://www.aacu.org/leap/hip.cfm.

79. Carnegie Endowment for the Advancement of Teaching, "Statway," http:// www.carnegiefoundation.org/statway; and "Developmental Math," http://www. carnegiefoundation.org/developmental-math.

80. See, e.g., the state constitutions in Alabama, Arizona, Hawaii, Massachusetts, North Dakota, Utah, West Virginia, and Wisconsin.

81. See, e.g., Charles A. Dana Center, Complete College America, Inc., Education Commission of the States, Jobs for the Future, "Core Principles for Transforming Remedial Education: A Joint Statement," December 2012, http://www.complete college.org/docs/Remediation_Joint_Statement-Embargo.pdf.

82. Saul Geiser and Richard Atkinson, "Beyond the Master Plan: The Case for Restructuring Baccalaureate Education in California," Center for Studies in Higher Education, University of California, Berkeley, November 2010.

83. Ibid., 23.

84. Ibid., 1.

85. Florida College System Task Force, "The Florida College System: Assuring Postsecondary Access That Supports Florida's Future," Florida Department of Education, December 2008, http://www.fldoe.org/cc/pdf/CollegeSystemFinalReport.pdf, 6–12, and "Florida College Bachelor's Degree Programs," Florida Department of Education, http://www.fldoe.org/cc/students/bach_degree.asp.

86. Paul Fain, "Michigan Lets Community Colleges Issue Four-year Degrees, amid Controversy," *Inside Higher Education,* January 22, 2013.

87. Jennifer Gonzalez, "Go to Community College, Earn a Bachelor's Degree: Florida Likes that Combination," *Chronicle of Higher Education,* June 17, 2011, A1.

88. There is little research on the effects of hybrid programs on racial, ethnic, and economic stratification in higher education, but researchers have suggested that baccalaureate programs, in particular, are likely to attract more middle-class students to community colleges. See, e.g., Thomas Bailey and Vanessa Smith Morest, "Introduction: Defending the Community College Equity Agenda," in *Defending the Community College Equity Agenda,* ed. Thomas Bailey and Vanessa Smith Morest (Baltimore, Md.: Johns Hopkins University Press, 2006), 1–27, 14.

89. Laura Horn and Paul Skomsvold, "Community College Student Outcomes: 1994–2009," U.S. Department of Education, Institute of Education Sciences, and National Center for Education Statistics, November 2011, Tables 1-A, 5-A and 7-A, http://nces.ed.gov/pubs2012/2012253.pdf ; see also U.S. Department of Education, National Center for Education Statistics, *The Condition of Education 2003,* NCES 2003-067 (Washington, D.C.: U.S. Government Printing Office, 2003), 130, table 19-1, http://nces.ed.gov/programs/coe/2003/section3/tables/t19_1.asp.

90. U.S. Census Bureau Historical Times Series Tables, Table A-3, "Mean Earnings of Workers 18 Years and Over, by Educational Attainment, Race, Hispanic Origin, and Sex: 1975 to 2010," http://www.census.gov/hhes/socdemo/education/data/cps/historical/index.html.

91. *Partnerships That Promote Success: Transfer from Community Colleges to Selective Four-Year Institutions,* conference hosted by the Jack Kent Cooke Foundation, September 15–17, 2010, http://www.jkcf.org/grants/community-college-transfer/2010-conference/.

92. Bowen et al., *Crossing the Finish Line,* 141.

93. "Promising Practices in Statewide Articulation and Transfer Systems," Hezel Associates, Lumina Foundation for Education, and Western Interstate Commission for Higher Education, June 2010, http://www.wiche.edu/info/publications/PromisingPracticesGuide.pdf, ix, 16.

94. The Aspen Prize for Community College Excellence, 2011, 9, http://www.aspeninstitute.org/sites/default/files/content/docs/pubs/AspenPrize021312.pdf.

95. Gail Mellow, letter to the editor, "At Elite Colleges, Too Much Hubris," *New York Times,* March 13, 2012, A24.

96. University of California StatFinder, http://statfinder.ucop.edu/default.aspx.

97. Anthony P. Carnevale, Tamara Jayasundera, and Andrew H. Hanson, "Career and Technical Education: Five Ways that Pay," Georgetown University Center on Education and the Workforce, September 2012, 31.

98. Christopher Mullin, "Transfer: An Indispensable Part of the Community College Mission," American Association of Community Colleges Policy Brief, October 2012, 5.

99. "Honors Scholar Program: Benefits for Students," Highline Community College, http://flightline.highline.edu/honors/benefits.htm (accessed November 16, 2010).

100. "Making Excellence Inclusive: Community College Honors," *AAC&U News,* December 2007, http://www.aacu.org/aacu_news/AACUNews07/december07/feature.cfm (accessed November 16, 2010).

101. "Honors Scholar Program: Why a Community College Honors Program?" Highline Community College, http://flightline.highline.edu/honors/HONORS100/ToolKit2/why-a-community-college-program.html (accessed November 16, 2010).

102. "Admissions," The Honors College, Miami Dade College, http://www.mdc.edu/honorscollege/admissions.asp (accessed April 28, 2011), and "Maintenance Requirements," The Honors College, Miami Dade College, http://www.mdc.edu/honorscollege/about_maintainance.asp (accessed April 28, 2011).

103. Alexandria Holloway, "The Honors College in a Two-Year College Setting: Miami Dade College," in *The Honors College Phenomenon,* ed. Peter C. Sederberg (Lincoln, Neb.: University of Nebraska—Lincoln, 2008), 47, http://digitalcommons.unl.edu/nchcmono/4/ (accessed April 28, 2011).

104. Some "early college" programs are aimed at giving underprepared students a chance to experience college in order to prevent later difficulties in transition. These programs may be important innovations in and of themselves but they do not advance the concern outlined in this report, which relates to socioeconomic and racial stratification.

105. Tiffany Waits, J. Carl Setzer, and Laurie Lewis, *Dual Credit and Exam-Based Courses in U.S. Public High Schools: 2002–03* (Washington, D.C.: U.S. Department of Education, Institute of Education Sciences, April 2005), 8, Figure 2, http://nces. ed.gov/pubs2005/2005009.pdf (accessed June 27, 2011).

106. In a 2007 study of Florida high school students, for example, 45.5 percent of non-dual enrollment students in the sample received free/reduced price lunch at some point in middle school, compared to 23.0 percent of dual enrollment students (those students who took at least one dual enrollment course in high school). See Melinda Mechur Karp et al., "The Postsecondary Achievement of Participants in Dual Enrollment: An Analysis of Student Outcomes in Two States," National Research Center for Career and Technical Education, University of Minnesota, October 2007, 25, Table 1, http://ccrc.tc.columbia.edu/publications/dual-enrollment-student-outcomes.html.

107. Waits, Setzer, and Lewis, *Dual Credit and Exam-Based Courses in U.S. Public High Schools*, 14.

108. Ibid.

109. Goldrick-Rab and Kinsley, 111, 129.

110. See, e.g., William G. Bowen, Martin A. Kurzweil and Eugene M. Tobin, *Equity and Excellence in American Higher Education* (Charlottesville, Va.: University of Virginia Press, 2005), 105, Table 1.

111. Carnevale and Rose, "Socioeconomic Status, Race/Ethnicity, and Selective College Admissions," 148–49.

112. Caroline M. Hoxby and Christopher Avery, "The Missing 'One-Offs': The Hidden Supply of High-Achieving, Low Income Students," National Bureau of Economic Research Working Paper Series, December 2012.

113. See, e.g. Golden and Katz, *The Race between Education and Technology*.

114. Minorities in the study are defined as people who are not "single-race white and not Hispanic." See "Most Children Younger Than Age 1 Are Minorities," United States Census Bureau, May 17, 2012, http://www.census.gov/newsroom/releases/archives/population/cb12-90.html, and Carol Morello and Ted Mellnik, "Census: Minority Babies Are Now Majority in United States," *Washington Post,* May 17, 2012, http://www.washingtonpost.com/local/census-minority-babies-are-now-majority-in-united-states/2012/05/16/gIQA1WY8UU_story.html.

115. United States Census Bureau, *2008 National Population Projections: Summary Tables,* Table 12, "Projections of the Population by Age and Sex for the United States: 2010 to 2050," and Table 13, "Projections of the White Alone Population by Age and Sex for the United States: 2010 to 2050," http://www.census.gov/population/projections/data/national/2008/summarytables.html.

116. "Transfer and Completion: Graduation Rates," College Board, http://completionarch.collegeboard.org/completion/graduation-rates.

117. Jeremy Offenstein and Nancy Shulock, "Community College Student Outcomes: Limitations of the Integrated Postsecondary Education Data System (IPEDS) and Recommendations for Improvement," Institute for Higher Education Leadership and Policy, California State University, Sacramento, August 2009, 7–9, http://www.csus.edu/ihelp/PDFs/R_IPEDS_08-09.pdf.

Additional Comment of Arthur J. Rothkopf

I commend the work of the Task Force, Richard Kahlenberg, and the researchers who helped inform this work. The report is an important addition to understanding the role of community colleges and the economics of higher education. I am confident the report will be a valuable part of the ongoing policy discussions on the role of community colleges. While I am unable to sign the report for the reasons discussed below, there are several recommendations that I enthusiastically support.

The Task Force is on target in concluding that community colleges are critical to the strategy necessary to address America's skills and education gaps, which threaten our ability to compete in the global economy. Community colleges also are central to addressing the need for Americans to obtain a solid education and the skills to obtain meaningful, well-paying employment.

I strongly endorse the following recommendations of the Task Force:

1. *Establish Greater Transparency Regarding Public Financial Subsidies to Higher Education.* More information about public support for higher education will prove especially valuable to policy-makers as they consider options.
2. *Encourage the Growth of Redesigned Institutions.* This recommendation will encourage greater connections among two- and four-year institutions and attract a broader cross-section of students to the new schools model.
3. *Take Steps to Facilitate Community College Transfer.* In order to make this recommendation a reality, new policies are required to permit easier transfers of credits between community colleges and public and private four-year institutions.

4. *Encourage Innovation in Economically Inclusive Community College Honors Programs.* This recommendation is an important part of the effort to attract high-achieving students to community colleges. I would not focus on race but solely on socioeconomic factors. I do not believe that racial factors should be a focus of the Task Force report, but rather, the emphasis should be on economic stratification.

5. *Encourage Innovation in Early College Programs That Enhance Community College Diversity.* This recommendation should prove valuable in attracting high-achieving students to community colleges that are economically isolated. I would not favor federal funding of these efforts.

6. *Encourage Four-Year Institutions to Engage in Affirmative Action for Low-Income Students of All Races.* The current trend in this direction needs to be accelerated.

On the other hand, I do not favor the adoption of a federal government K–12, Title I–type program for community colleges, nor do I support the recommendation that federal government funding for honors, early college, and other programs be directed first to those community colleges with few middle-class students. All community colleges should be treated alike.

The U.S. government is currently at a point where the utmost fiscal austerity must be imposed on current programs, and especially on significant new programs. The Title I program for K–12 not only is very expensive, but its outcomes are far from clear. Certainly there is widespread acknowledgement that current results from K–12 public education fall far short of what we have a right to expect. Incorporating the Title I approach into funding community colleges seems questionable, unless the data strongly supports it. I do not believe that is the case here. One example is Figure 6 of the Task Force report, which indicates that per-pupil public funding of public community colleges is slightly higher than per-pupil public funding of the public master's schools. It does not appear from this chart that community colleges are being short-changed in relation to their four-year public sister institutions.

The Task Force recommendation supporting a Title I approach to community college funding suggests that outcomes be taken into account in determining where the funding is directed. This is a commendable suggestion, but highly doubtful in application. Federal data on postsecondary students is currently so confusing and often unavailable as to make this suggestion impractical. Until we have a federal unit record system covering all students, this recommendation could not be properly implemented.

If more funding for community colleges is to be considered by the Congress, which I believe requires much more persuasive data, consideration should be given to "paying for" any new program by eliminating those federal tax credits that benefit those who would attend college in any event. As pointed out in the Task Force report, these tax credits can benefit families with income of up to $180,000 a year. Another potential source of revenue would be the denial of a federal tax deduction for contributions to the intercollegiate athletic programs of colleges and universities. These programs provide no benefit to the educational missions of their institutions.

Background Papers

Community Colleges in Context:

Exploring Financing of
Two- and Four-Year Institutions

SANDY BAUM and CHARLES KUROSE

As we emerge from the Great Recession in the United States, assuring adequate postsecondary educational opportunities to all who can benefit should be high on our list of public policy priorities. Community colleges—which educate a disproportionate share of students from low-income backgrounds, of adults returning to hone their skills for the labor market, and of students in need of strong academic and social supports to be able to do college-level work—deserve particular attention. Since these institutions depend more than other colleges on appropriations from state and local governments, smaller public budgets have meant they have seen declines in per-student revenues and expenditures, exacerbating the difficulties of meeting student needs and of achieving acceptable completion rates.

Both equity and efficiency considerations demand that we gain greater understanding of the reasons and potential remedies for the disappointing educational outcomes of the students served by community colleges. Our economy depends on an increasingly skilled labor force, and future growth will necessarily come from historically underrepresented populations. As achieving a middle-class standard of living becomes less and less possible without some sort of college credential, neglecting the needs of community college students relegates a large group of people to lives of unnecessary hardship.

This paper provides necessary background for developing policies to strengthen community colleges. We review the history and growth of the sector and examine the available data on revenues, expenditures, salaries, student subsidies, and the subsidies that institutions receive through tax exemption. In the absence of adequate data to distinguish expenditures on different types of students within institutions, we perform a hypothetical exercise to compare spending on community college students to spending on lower-division undergraduates in other sectors. Finally, we discuss the relevant considerations for determining equitable and efficient funding and we suggest ways that our ability to make those difficult decisions could be improved. There is no doubt that supporting the success of community college students requires much more than adequate funding for the students and their institutions. But without adequate funding, significant progress is unlikely.

BACKGROUND

Goals of Community Colleges

The history of community colleges dates back to the high school–based Joliet Junior College in Illinois, developed in 1901.[1] But the community college system as we know it has its roots in the report of the 1947 President's Commission on Higher Education, better known as the Truman Commission, which argued that higher education is necessary to the development of a democratic citizenry and should be more accessible. "Equal opportunity for all persons, to the maximum of their individual abilities and without regard to economic status, race, creed, color, sex, national origin, or ancestry is a major goal of American democracy. Only an informed, thoughtful, tolerant people can develop and maintain a free society."[2]

The Truman Commission believed that community colleges should be located so that they would be geographically accessible to most people. It believed that many more students could and should complete two years of undergraduate study than would earn four-year degrees. Re-conceptualizing junior colleges as community colleges, the Truman Commission introduced this term into the national vocabulary because of the importance of vocational education supplementing the transfer role of junior colleges and of the integration of this new type of institution into local communities.

Community College Enrollment

In the 1960s, the community college sector began to expand dramatically, and many more adults, including many women and people of color, enrolled in college. Community colleges were no longer just junior colleges—stepping-stones to four-year colleges—but were institutions providing the skills many needed to become productive members of the labor force. Between 1963 and 2010, fall enrollment at community colleges grew from around 700,000 students to more than 7 million. That increase corresponds to an average annual growth rate of 5.0 percent, which is considerably higher than the 3.2 percent annual rate of growth in fall enrollment experienced across all sectors of higher education. Over that time period, the community college sector's share of total fall enrollment rose from 15 percent to 34 percent.[3]

Many students enrolling in community colleges are returning to higher education after a break, but about 40 percent of first-time degree-seeking students enroll in this sector. This percentage grew rapidly, from 31 percent in 1966 to 51 percent in 1975, and held steady at about 50 percent through the early 1980s. At that point, other sectors began increasing their shares of first-time enrollment and two-year public colleges' share of beginning students declined to 37 percent by the mid-2000s, and stood at 39 percent in fall 2010.[4] The community college sector's share of first-time enrollment is higher than its share of total fall enrollment because students spend more years enrolled in four-year than in two-year institutions.

Composition of the Student Body

The demographic profile at community colleges looks very different from that of the student bodies at other types of postsecondary institutions. Public two-year college students today are disproportionately non-white. Hispanic students are overrepresented in the sector, constituting 18 percent of the students at community colleges but only 13 percent of all students at degree-granting institutions. In 2010, almost half of all Hispanic college students across the country were enrolled at community colleges.[5] Black students are not overrepresented at community colleges, but instead they enroll in disproportionate numbers at for-profit institutions. As Table 1 indicates (page 76), the share of black students in total enrollment at for-profit institutions (29 percent) was

Bridging the Higher Education Divide

TABLE 1
Fall Enrollment in Degree-Granting Institutions by Racial/Ethnic Group, 2010

	Total	Public Two-Year	Public Four-Year	Private Nonprofit Four-Year	For-Profit
White	61%	57%	64%	66%	49%
Black	14%	15%	12%	12%	29%
Hispanic	13%	18%	11%	8%	14%
Asian/Pacific Islander	6%	6%	7%	6%	4%
Other	6%	4%	7%	8%	4%

Source: Thomas D. Snyder and Sally A. Dillow, *Digest of Education Statistics 2011* (Washington, D.C.: U.S. Department of Education, National Center for Education Statistics, 2012), table 241.

more than twice as high as the share of black students in total postsecondary enrollment (14 percent) in 2010.

Both students who are older than traditional college age and those who are younger are over-represented at community colleges. In 2011, when fall enrollment at community colleges was 39 percent of the total, 66 percent of students under 18 years of age and 48 percent of students aged 25 or older were enrolled at community colleges.[6] It is perhaps unsurprising that so many younger students enroll at community colleges, since community colleges are located close to home and offer a comparatively wide range of degree- and non-degree programs, in particular for vocational training. Moreover, many of the younger students are participating in dual-enrollment programs with their high schools. For adults, at least part of the appeal of community colleges is that community colleges are well equipped to accommodate the busy schedules of those with full-time jobs and families to care for.

Another distinguishing feature of community colleges is their high rate of part-time enrollment. More than half (54 percent) of all students enrolling part-time did so at community colleges in 2010. In contrast, the community college sector claimed only 23 percent of all full-time students that year. Within the community college sector, part-time students are in the majority, with 59 percent of community college students enrolling part-time in 2010.[7]

Community college students tend to come from lower income backgrounds than do students in the other sectors. Figure 1 shows the

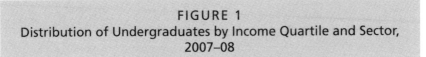

FIGURE 1
Distribution of Undergraduates by Income Quartile and Sector, 2007–08

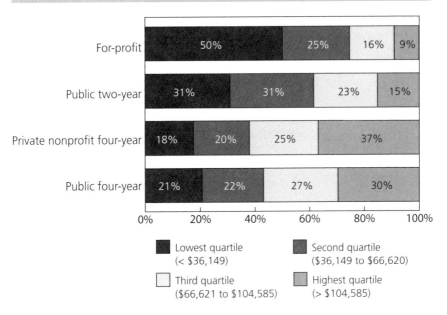

Source: U.S. Department of Education, Institute of Education Sciences, National Center for Education Statistics, 2007–08 National Postsecondary Student Aid Study (NPSAS:08).

distribution of dependent undergraduate students across income quartiles within each sector in 2008.[8] About one-third of the dependent students enrolling at community colleges (and about half of those at for-profit institutions) were from the lowest family income quartile in 2008, compared to about 20 percent of the dependent students at public and private nonprofit four-year colleges and universities. As shown in Figure 2, however, dependent students constituted only 24 percent of undergraduate enrollment in the for-profit sector and 43 percent at community colleges. These figures compare to 66 percent at private nonprofit four-year institutions and 69 percent at public four-year institutions.[9]

Degrees and Certificates at Community Colleges

Most programs at community colleges lead to associate's degrees or to certificates of varying program duration. As Table 2 indicates,

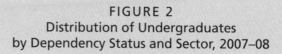

FIGURE 2
Distribution of Undergraduates by Dependency Status and Sector, 2007–08

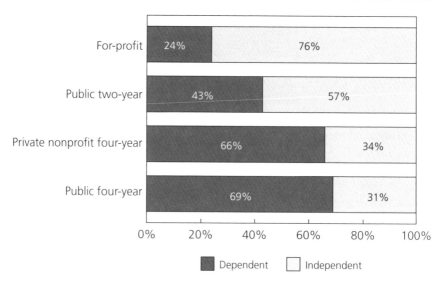

Source: U.S. Department of Education, Institute of Education Sciences, National Center for Education Statistics, 2007–08 National Postsecondary Student Aid Study (NPSAS:08).

TABLE 2
Associate's Degrees and Certificates by Sector, 2010

	Associate's Degrees	Certificates of Two but Less Than Four Years	Certificates of One but Less Than Two Years	Certificates of Less Than One Year	Percentage of Total
Public four-year	12.0%	12.3%	3.8%	7.2%	9.4%
Private nonprofit four-year	4.3%	5.9%	1.8%	1.2%	3.2%
For-profit four-year	13.4%	2.8%	6.8%	2.6%	9.7%
Public two-year	62.1%	57.4%	53.7%	71.6%	62.6%
Private nonprofit two-year	0.7%	0.6%	0.6%	0.7%	0.7%
For-profit two-year	7.5%	21.0%	33.3%	16.7%	14.4%
Percentage of all awards	58.9%	0.8%	18.6%	21.6%	100%

Source: U.S. Department of Education, Institute of Education Sciences, National Center for Education Statistics, Integrated Postsecondary Education Data System (IPEDS).

community colleges award the majority of the associate's degrees and certificates, including a particularly large share of certificates for programs that are less than one year in duration.[10]

The number of certificates awarded across all of higher education has been growing rapidly in recent years, having risen from about 550,000 in 2000 to nearly one million a decade later, and for many students they are a cost-effective and relatively quick path to better jobs, higher wages, and further postsecondary degrees.[11] A recent study by Anthony Carnevale, Stephen Rose, and Andrew Hanson carefully examines the pay-offs to this increasingly popular postsecondary option.[12]

Certificate programs are usually oriented toward vocational or occupation-specific training. The community college sector, where a large number of certificates are awarded, is therefore a common destination for students seeking to develop those types of skills. Some people see community colleges mainly as stepping-stones to further education, while others see them principally as destinations in and of themselves that offer shorter-term, often (though not exclusively) vocationally oriented forms of postsecondary education. The current reality is that community colleges serve both of these purposes. They produce many more associate's degrees and certificates than does any other sector, but many community college students also move on to bachelor's programs at four-year institutions. According to the National Student Clearinghouse, 26 percent of the students who began their studies at community colleges in 2006 had transferred to four-year institutions within five years.[13] For a thorough account of the multi-faceted nature of the community college, see Kevin Dougherty's book, *The Contradictory College*.[14]

Variation across States

The role of community colleges varies considerably across state systems of higher education. Nationally, about one-third of all postsecondary students—and almost half of all of those enrolled in the public sector—attend community colleges; but in 2010, the share of postsecondary students enrolled in community colleges ranged from lows of 3 percent in Alaska and 10 percent in Nevada to highs of 58 percent in California and 61 percent in Wyoming. In thirteen states, less than one quarter of all undergraduates were enrolled in this sector, while in six states, more than half of all undergraduates were in community colleges.[15]

Tuition prices at community colleges also vary widely across the country. In 2012–13, the sticker price for a full-time community college student was $1,418 in California and $1,537 in New Mexico, compared to $6,790 in Vermont and $6,752 in New Hampshire. The average community college tuition was only 15 percent of the average tuition at public four-year institutions in California, 23 percent in Arizona, and 26 percent in Texas. In contrast, those ratios were 68 percent in New York and 73 percent in South Dakota.[16]

While many factors other than price affect enrollment decisions—and prices and institutional patterns and structures are themselves determined by state policies and populations—there is a correlation between prices and enrollment patterns. In the five states with the highest community college tuition in 2010–11—South Dakota, Massachusetts, Minnesota, New Hampshire, and Vermont—the average state's price was $5,328 and, on average, 24 percent of undergraduate fall enrollment was in community colleges. In the five states with the lowest community college tuition—Arizona, North Carolina, Texas, California, and New Mexico—the average state's price was $1,551 and, on average, 52 percent of undergraduates were enrolled in community colleges in the fall. Figure 3 plots each state's community college enrollment rate against its average community college tuition during the 2010–11 academic year.[17]

COMMUNITY COLLEGE FINANCE

Are Comparisons of Per-Student Costs across Institutions Reliable?

Available data on institutional revenues and expenditures are unfortunately not adequate for reliable comparisons of expenditures on specific activities across sectors. It is also not possible to precisely separate expenditures on graduate students from expenditures on undergraduates—much less spending on lower- versus upper-level undergraduates. A major problem with the available data is that the counts of students include only those registered for credit. Community colleges offer many non-credit programs. While the revenues generated and expenditures devoted to these programs are included in the totals, the participating students are not. This problem biases per-student revenues and expenditures upward relative to those computed for four-year institutions.

In addition, there are significant differences in the costs of educating students in different disciplines, regardless of the types of institutions in which they are enrolled. Thus, differences between institutions in the mix of available programs make a large difference in the cost of educating

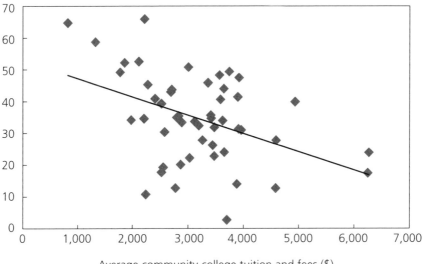

FIGURE 3
Average Community College Tuition and the
Percentage of Undergraduates Attending Community Colleges,
Across States, 2010–11

Percentage of undergraduates attending community colleges

Average community college tuition and fees ($)

Source: Thomas D. Snyder and Sally A. Dillow, *Digest of Education Statistics 2011* (Washington, D.C.: U.S. Department of Education, National Center for Education Statistics, 2012), table 226; Sandy Baum and Jennifer Ma, "Trends in College Pricing 2012," College Board, 2012.

students. According to a National Center for Education Statistics (NCES) report based on the Delaware Cost Study, disciplinary mix explains most of the variation in instructional costs across institutions. For example, instructional costs in mechanical engineering are about three times as high as those in English. The time members of the faculty spend teaching, the other responsibilities they have, and the number of students they teach also make a significant difference in per-student costs.[18]

Within the community college sector, technical occupational training is much more expensive than liberal arts education. At one college in upstate New York, the cost per credit hour and per degree granted for a student in the health science and technical areas is three to four times higher than it is for a typical liberal arts student.[19] Engineering programs spend much more per student than do humanities programs. Unfortunately, the institutional-level data in the NCES' Integrated Postsecondary Education Data System (IPEDS)—on which most estimates of institutional costs, revenues, and subsidies rely—do not allow for accurate comparisons at the program level.

In addition to disciplinary mix, differences in missions across institutions make per-student figures unreliable as estimates of the difference between the amount spent on students enrolled in community colleges and the amount spent on those pursuing their first two years of undergraduate education at four-year institutions. There is broad agreement, however, that it costs more to educate upper-division undergraduates than lower-division undergraduates, and more yet to educate graduate students.

Why should there be cost differences? One issue is that teaching faculties in universities include graduate students in addition to part-time, full-time, adjunct, tenure-track, and tenured faculty members, instructors, and assistant, associate, and full professors. The tenured professors working with graduate students are paid more than the assistant professors teaching juniors and seniors, and much more than the graduate students staffing entry-level courses. Teaching loads vary considerably, both within and between institutions. Another issue is that instructional expenditures include departmental (unfunded) research, which arguably has minimal impact on the quality of lower-level courses. Class sizes are also generally larger for introductory level courses.

The general consensus in the literature is that it costs about one-and-a-half times as much to educate upper-level undergraduates as it does to educate lower-level undergraduates, and about three times more to educate graduate students. These ratios lead some researchers to estimate that costs per lower-division student at four-year public universities are similar to costs per community college student—or slightly lower, or slightly higher.[20] Even if expenditures per student are lower at community colleges, because community college students almost always pay lower tuition than do four-year college students, lower costs per student do not necessarily imply lower subsidies per student.

A recent attempt to compare spending on students in two- and four-year public colleges comes from Richard Romano and Yenni M. Djajalaksana.[21] Because their goal is to determine whether it would relieve pressure on state budgets if more students were to begin their studies at community colleges, the authors use public master's universities—the most likely alternative institutions for community college students—as the main comparison group. They estimate that, after subtracting the research and public service components, education and general expenditures per student were almost $2,000 (22 percent) higher at the median public master's university than at the median public two-year college in 2005. However, adjusting for spending one-and-a-half times as much on upper-division as on lower-division students, expenditures per student were about $1,800 (20 percent) *less* in the four-year institutions.

With these caveats in mind, we begin by comparing data on the expenditures, revenue sources, and institutional subsidies per full-time equivalent (FTE) student, as well as faculty salaries, in the community college sector to other institutional sectors. These analyses are based on data from the Delta Cost Project, a multi-year project at the American Institutes for Research that has used data from IPEDS to create a large set of variables detailing institutional characteristics that can be compared over time.

Following discussion of these data, we focus on developing a constructive approach to making the comparisons more meaningful. Assumptions about actual—and appropriate—spending differences on students at different levels are critical to drawing conclusions about the funding of students in community colleges and other institutions. In the absence of a clear method for estimating the appropriate ratios, we estimate what the ratios would have to be for the levels of revenue and expenditures at community colleges to be equivalent to the revenues and expenditures for lower-division students at four-year public universities.

Expenditures

This section discusses the types of expenditures that are directly related to the actual educating of students. In the Delta Cost Project data, there are three expenditure items that, taken together, constitute total education and related (E&R) spending. They are instruction, student services, and the "education share" of spending on a basket of other budget items—academic support, institutional support, and operations and maintenance.[22]

Even when only looking at E&R expenditures, large differences exist across institutions, as shown in Figure 4 (page 84). At community colleges, since 1989, E&R expenditures have grown at an average annual rate of 0.8 percent after adjusting for inflation, reaching $9,348 per FTE student in 2009. In every year during that time period, community colleges had lower E&R expenditures per FTE student than did each of the other sectors (even without considering non-credit enrollees). Indeed, in every one of those years and in every subcategory of

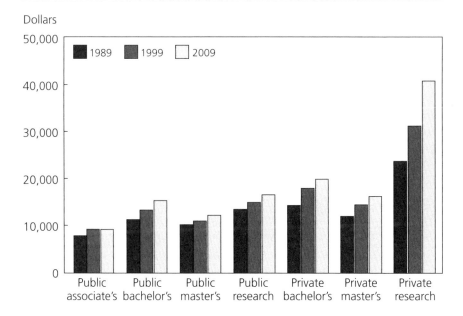

FIGURE 4
Total Education and Related (E&R) Expenditures per FTE Student by Carnegie Sector, 1989, 1999, and 2009 (in 2009 dollars)

Source: The Delta Cost Project, American Institutes for Research; calculations by the authors.

TABLE 3
Total Education and Related (E&R) Expenditures per FTE Student by Carnegie Sector, 1989, 1999, and 2009 (in 2009 dollars)

	1989	*1999*	*2009*
Public associate's	$7,999	$9,383	$9,348
Public bachelor's	$11,443	$13,480	$15,504
Public master's	$10,376	$11,152	$12,360
Public research	$13,638	$15,112	$16,731
Private bachelor's	$14,462	$18,143	$20,079
Private master's	$12,149	$14,612	$16,391
Private research	$23,911	$31,405	$41,019

Source: The Delta Cost Project, American Institutes for Research; calculations by the authors.

E&R spending—instruction, student services, and the "education share" of other expenditures—community colleges spent less per FTE than did each of the other sectors. (The one exception was in 1996, when community colleges spent $1,000 per FTE student on student services, compared to $965 at public master's institutions.) The gap between E&R expenditures per FTE at private research universities and E&R expenditures per FTE in each of the other sectors has increased markedly since 2000; the gap between public master's universities and public associate's colleges has not.

Revenue

In addition to spending less, community colleges also bring in less revenue per FTE student (even without considering non-credit enrollments) than do institutions in any of the other sectors. Figure 5 (page 86) shows that in all sectors, revenue per FTE student increased from 1989 to 2009.[23] Revenue per FTE student grew at an average annual rate of 1.2 percent at community colleges, compared to 0.9 percent in public master's institutions and 1.5 percent in public research universities.

In 2009, 58 percent of the revenues of community colleges came from state and local appropriations.[24] This compares to 45 percent, 43 percent, and 34 percent in the public bachelor's, public master's, and public research sectors, respectively. (State and local appropriations to private institutions are extremely small.) State appropriations constituted a much larger portion of the budgets in all four public sectors twenty years ago than they do today, but community colleges have been most dependent on this source of funding as far back as the data go.

At community colleges, the decrease in funding from state and local appropriations has been accompanied by a rise in tuition revenue per FTE student, net of institutional grant aid. In 2009, community colleges' net tuition revenue per FTE student stood at $2,907, which was considerably lower than the same figure for any other sector—public or private—yet still represents a steady average annual growth rate of 3.1 percent since 1987. Unlike most private institutions and many public four-year institutions, community colleges don't benefit significantly from private gifts, investment income, and endowment earnings.

Salaries

The funding levels of community colleges are reflected in much higher student/faculty and student/staff ratios than those found in public

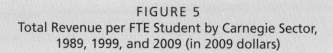

FIGURE 5
Total Revenue per FTE Student by Carnegie Sector,
1989, 1999, and 2009 (in 2009 dollars)

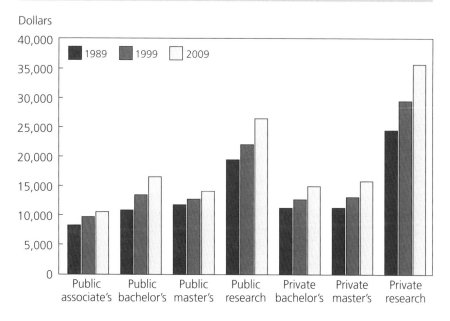

Source: The Delta Cost Project, American Institutes for Research; calculations by the authors.

TABLE 4
Total Revenue per FTE Student by Carnegie Sector,
1989, 1999, and 2009 (in 2009 dollars)

	1989	*1999*	*2009*
Public associate's	$8,398	$9,817	$10,675
Public bachelor's	$10,963	$13,546	$16,648
Public master's	$11,883	$12,839	$14,186
Public research	$19,562	$22,132	$26,561
Private bachelor's	$11,335	$12,779	$15,048
Private master's	$11,373	$13,187	$15,911
Private research	$24,558	$29,559	$35,771

Source: The Delta Cost Project, American Institutes for Research; calculations by the authors.

TABLE 5
Composition of Revenues at Public Associate's Institutions,
1989, 1999, and 2009

	1989	1999	2009
Net tuition revenue	18%	22%	27%
State and local appropriations	72%	65%	58%
State and local grants and contracts	7%	8%	9%
Federal revenue net of Pell	5%	6%	7%

Source: The Delta Cost Project, American Institutes for Research; calculations by the authors.

TABLE 6
Composition of Revenues at Public Institutions, 2009

	Public Associate's	Public Master's	Public Research	Public Bachelor's
Net tuition revenue	27%	43%	32%	27%
State and local appropriations	58%	43%	34%	45%
State and local grants and contracts	9%	8%	12%	6%
Federal revenue net of Pell	7%	7%	22%	23%

Source: The Delta Cost Project, American Institutes for Research; calculations by the authors.

four-year colleges. In fall 2009, community colleges averaged 22 FTE students per FTE faculty member, compared to a ratio of 15-to-1 in public four-year institutions. When all staff were considered, the ratios were 10-to-1 at public two-year institutions and 5-to-1 at public four-year institutions. Given the variation in funding levels across states, it is not surprising that the student/faculty and student/staff ratios also differ considerably. California, which has the lowest community college prices and the largest fraction of students enrolled in that sector, had a student/faculty ratio of 27-to-1 at community colleges in 2009 compared to 17-to-1 in the public four-year sector. New Hampshire, which has the highest tuition levels, had a ratio of 9-to-1 at community colleges compared to 18-to-1 in the four-year sector.[25]

Comparisons of faculty salaries between the two- and four-year sectors are problematic because the job qualifications and responsibilities

FIGURE 6
Average Full-Time Faculty Salary Relative to the
Public Associate's Sector, 1991, 1999, and 2009

FT faculty salary relative to the public associate's sector

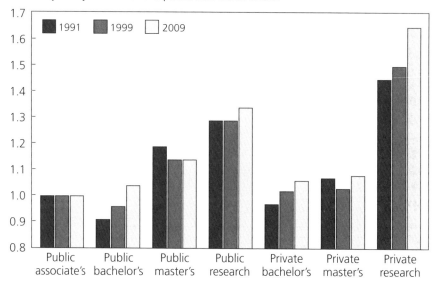

Source: The Delta Cost Project, American Institutes for Research; calculations by the authors.

are quite different. In fall 2003, when 73 percent of faculty in public four-year colleges and universities had PhDs, only 18 percent of those teaching in community colleges had this level of education. For 17 percent of community college faculty members, the highest level of education was a bachelor's degree or lower.[26] This was the case for only 3 percent of those teaching in public four-year colleges. Faculty at community colleges spend about 78 percent of their work time teaching, compared to 65 percent for those at public master's universities and 58 percent for faculty overall.[27] Research accounts for a significant portion of the time of university faculty, but is generally not part of the job description of community college faculty. However, community college faculty members may well spend more time on curricular development, student support, and pedagogical development than do faculty members at other institutions.

As shown in Figure 6, in both 1991 and 1999, the ratio of the average full-time faculty salary at public research institutions to that at community

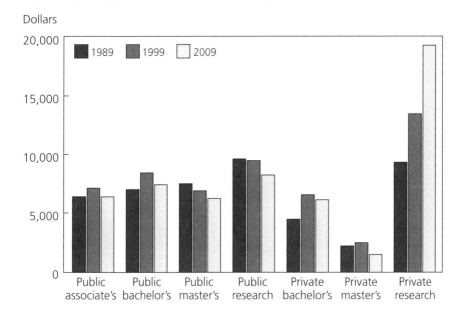

FIGURE 7
Average Subsidy per FTE Student, 1989, 1999, and 2009
(in 2009 dollars)

Source: The Delta Cost Project, American Institutes for Research; calculations by the authors.

colleges was 1.29. By 2009, salaries in public research universities averaged 34 percent more than those at community colleges. However, the ratio of the average salary at public master's universities to that at community colleges was 1.19 in 1991, and 1.14 in both 1999 and 2009.

Subsidies

Most students are subsidized, with their tuition and fees covering less than the full cost of their education. The difference between average E&R spending and average net tuition (net of institutional grant aid) is a measure of the level of the average subsidy per student. Figure 7 shows this measure across sectors and over time.

The average subsidy per FTE student at community colleges ($6,440 in 2009) compares favorably to that of private master's institutions ($6,294). However, the average subsidy per student in 2009 was $8,293

FIGURE 8
The Average Subsidy's Share of Total E&R Expenditures,
1989, 1999, and 2009

Average subsidy's share of total E&R expenditures

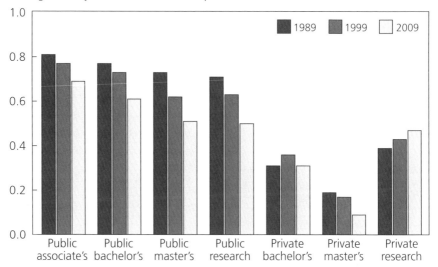

Source: The Delta Cost Project, American Institutes for Research; calculations by the authors.

at public research universities and $7,469 at public bachelor's colleges. At community colleges, the average subsidy per FTE student has fluctuated over time, but in 2009, community colleges were subsidizing students' educations to roughly the same extent as they had in 1989. There is much more variation in subsidy levels across types of private institutions. In 2009, the average student in a private research university enjoyed a subsidy of $19,342, while the figure for private master's universities was only $1,528.

Due to the considerable differences in total E&R expenditures between sectors, the differences in dollar subsidies do not necessarily correspond to differences in the shares of E&R expenditures that are covered by the average subsidy. That share is displayed for each sector in Figure 8. In every year for which data are available, the average subsidy has covered a larger share of E&R expenditures at community colleges than in any other sector, despite having gradually declined from a high of 81 percent in 1989 to a low of 69 percent in 2009. The average subsidy's share of E&R expenditures declined over that time period in all of the public sectors, but to a greater extent at research, master's, and bachelor's institutions than at community colleges. The large share of E&R expenditures that is covered by the average subsidy at community colleges translates directly into a low share being covered by net tuition. In other words, students bear a smaller share of the cost of their education at community colleges than in any other sector.

Subsidies to Private Colleges through Tax Exemption

As the data about subsidies discussed above indicate, students enrolled in private research universities receive significantly larger subsidies than students enrolled in either two- or four-year public colleges. Seminal studies on student subsidies by Gordon Winston in the 1990s indicated that students in the most selective, best-endowed private colleges received subsides averaging about $23,000 in 1995—far more than the total cost of education in public institutions.[28] This pattern persists today, but most of these subsidies are from private funds. From a policy perspective, it is really the allocation of public subsidies that is most relevant.

Not visible in the subsidy data discussed above are the savings enjoyed by private nonprofit institutions as a result of their nonprofit status—their exemption from property, sales, and income taxes, as well as the tax deductions from which donors benefit. Public colleges also benefit from this tax-exempt status, but the benefits flow primarily to four-year colleges, particularly the flagship institutions with foundations and loyal alumni. How best to estimate the value of these subsidies depends on what type of tax might most reasonably be imposed if the tax exemption were lifted.

Endowment Earnings. If private colleges and universities were for-profit entities, they would pay taxes on their profits. The logical way to measure profits would be in terms of increases in net worth—essentially, increases in endowment value. In 2010, private colleges held a total of about $245 billion in endowment assets. However, thirteen universities held half of these assets.[29] The total value of the assets held by these thirteen universities declined from $154 billion in 2008 to $115 billion in 2009, and increased to $124 billion in 2010.[30] In other words, a tax on "profits" would not yield predictable revenues.

The thirteen wealthiest institutions had endowment assets averaging almost $640,000 per FTE student in 2010—generating over $30,000 per student per year in revenues. However, most students receive much lower subsidies from endowments. In 2010, the median student in a private doctoral university benefited from $58,800 in endowment assets—or less than $3,000 in annual revenue. For students in private master's universities, the figure was $10,410 of assets (about $500 per student per year), and for those in private bachelor's colleges, it was $24,650 of assets (about $1,200 per student per year).[31]

It might be possible to impose a tax on the income from college endowments. If we assume that annual earnings average about 5 percent of asset values, all private college endowments would generate a total of about $12 billion in annual incomes. With federal corporate income tax rates ranging from 15 percent to 35 percent, a tax on these incomes could raise between $2 billion and $4 billion per year. Using a rate of return of 8 percent would yield tax revenues of $3 billion to $7 billion per year.

A 2007 Congressional Research Service (CRS) report indicated that taxing endowment income at the 35 percent corporate tax rate could yield about $18 billion in tax revenues.[32] However, the path of the economy in the intervening years suggests that this estimate is too high. After declining precipitously in 2008, the total value of private college endowments had recovered to about 93 percent of the 2007 value by 2010.[33] Starting with the $340 billion asset value that is the basis of the CRS calculation and adjusting for the decline yields a total current value of about $316 billion. The 15.3 percent return for 2007 reported by CRS was an anomaly. According to the National Association of College and University Business Officers and Commonfund Institute, the average ten-year return of U.S. higher education endowments and affiliated foundations for the period ending June 30, 2011, was 5.6 percent.[34] Taxing an annual 5.6 percent return of $17.7 billion at 35 percent would yield tax revenues of about $6.2 billion.

No such tax on income applies to museums, hospitals, or other endowed nonprofit institutions. Moreover, this would be a tax on endowment earnings—not a tax on profits. Because institutional expenditures tend to equal total revenues—after allowing for maintenance of the purchasing power of the endowment—taxing profits would be unlikely to generate significant revenues.

Public universities held a total of about $74 billion in endowment assets in 2010, which was about $13,000 in assets or just over $600 in revenue per FTE student per year. As is the case in the private sector, these assets are highly concentrated in a few institutions. Nine universities have one-third of the endowment assets, and the wealthiest twenty-one have one-half.[35] While the largest endowment per student generates almost $9,000 per student per year, the tenth largest generates just over $2,000 per student.

Most tax-exempt private foundations are subject to an excise tax of 2 percent on their net investment income. This is the amount by which income, dividends and rents, and net capital gains exceed the costs associated with generating that income. In other words, the tax rate on foundation income is much lower than the tax rate on corporate profits, but the tax is on income—not the amount by which income exceeds costs. A 2 percent tax on the endowment income of private colleges would generate $240 million to $400 million per year.

Property Taxes. Nonprofit colleges are also exempt from property taxes. The fact that many institutions make payments to local governments in lieu of property taxes, and the variation in property values and in property tax rates across regions, make estimating the associated subsidy virtually impossible.

Tax Exemption for Donations and Exclusion of Interest on Bonds for Private Education Facilities. The absence of tax revenues on interest paid by educational institutions on facilities bonds cost the federal government about $2.1 billion in 2011.[36] The tax expenditure for the deductibility of charitable contributions to educational institutions is about $3.5 billion. Not all of these benefits accrue to colleges—or to private colleges. But these two provisions could contribute about $4 billion in tax subsidy to private colleges.

Sales Taxes. Nonprofit colleges and universities are exempt from sales taxes. There is no simple way to estimate the value of this exemption.

If we assume the most extreme case—that private colleges receive about $10 billion per year in tax subsidies, this amounts to a subsidy of approximately $3,100 for each of the 3.2 million FTE students enrolled in this sector. However, as noted, these subsidies are concentrated on a small percentage of the students in the sector. The thirty-four private institutions with endowment assets per student (including both undergraduate and graduate students) exceeding $300,000 in 2010 enrolled about 178,000 of the sector's 3.2 million FTE students—less than 6 percent. The students in the other 2,900 private institutions receive much smaller subsidies than these lucky few. As discussed above and developed further below, it is also likely that graduate students enjoy a disproportionate share of the subsidy, and upper-division undergraduates benefit more than lower-division undergraduates.

Accounting for Differences in the Level of Students

The previous sections have compared per-student revenues and expenditures across institutions that educate very different mixes of students. In addition to important disciplinary variation, community colleges educate only lower-division undergraduates while all four-year institutions also enroll upper-division undergraduates and universities enroll master's, doctoral, and professional students as well. As a result, simple per-student comparisons exaggerate the relative lack of resources at community colleges.

The key question in determining whether more money is spent on lower-division undergraduates at universities than on community college students is the ratio of spending per upper-division undergraduate and graduate student to spending per lower-division undergraduate in universities. If advanced students benefit from a very disproportionate share, then spending on lower-division undergraduates at universities and community college students may be similar—or the latter may, as some researchers have concluded, even be higher. Unfortunately, the data necessary to establish the actual ratio are not available. So in order to gain more insight into the resources devoted to community college students relative to those in other institutions, instead of taking the common approach that assumes spending in other institutions is one-and-a-half times higher, we engage here in a hypothetical exercise.

We take the approach of asking what the ratio of spending on advanced students to spending on lower-division undergraduates would have to be for per-student expenditures on lower-division undergraduates in other sectors to be as low as they are at community colleges.[37] In other words, we start with the average costs of education at community colleges. Knowing the approximate number of students in other sectors who are at the first- and second-year level, we can estimate how much these institutions would be spending on this group if they were spending the same amount per student as community colleges spend. All of their remaining expenditures would then be devoted to advanced students, and we can calculate the implied level of spending per advanced student. If this exercise suggested that they would be spending the same amount on students at all levels, we would conclude that this is unlikely and that in reality, they are probably spending *less* per lower-division student than community colleges are, while focusing more funding on the more advanced students. If the exercise suggested that they would be spending six times as much per advanced student as per lower-division student, we would conclude that this is also unlikely and that in reality, they are probably spending considerably *more* per lower division student than community colleges are, while still having resources left over to spend even more at the upper levels.

A simpler example may help to clarify the concept of this exercise. Suppose we were interested in estimating how much coed colleges spend on women's athletics relative to the amount spent at women's colleges, but the data would not allow a clear separation between men's and women's sports. We could easily take total expenditures on athletics at women's colleges and divide by the number of students to find expenditures per woman. In Table 7, the $500 of total athletic expenditures on 100 women equals $5 per woman.

For the coed institution, we could assume that spending on men is, for example, twice as high as spending on women, and then find out how much would be left over for the women. But if we wanted to avoid choosing a rather arbitrary number, we could instead assume that the coed institution, like the women's college, spends $5 per woman. In the simple example in Table 7, for Coed College A, this would require

TABLE 7
Example of Thought Experiment about Athletic Spending

	Women's College	Coed College A	Coed College B
Number of women	100	50	50
Number of men	0	100	100
Total athletic spending	$500	$1,500	$750
Athletic spending per student	$5	$10	$5
Athletic spending on women at $5 per	$500	$250	$250
Remaining athletic spending	$0	$1,250	$500
Implied spending per man	$0	$12.5	$5
Implied male/female ratio	—	2.5	1.0

$250 of the $1,500 athletics budget, leaving $1,250 for the 100 men—
or $12.50 per man. In other words, if Coed College A spent the same
amount per woman as the women's college, they would be spending 2.5
times as much per man as per woman—a ratio that is higher than might
be expected or accepted. It is more likely that this college is spending
more than $5 per woman and less than $12.50 per man.

Coed College B provides a different example. Its athletic budget is
$750 and if $250 is going to women, there is $500 left over for the 100
men. The $5 per man would be exactly equal to the $5 per woman. This
is also unlikely, given the nature of football and other men's sports, so
we might assume that this college is actually spending less than $5 per
woman—and that female athletes would enjoy more resources at the
women's college.

In the spirit of this example, we have calculated what the ratio of
E&R spending on advanced students to E&R spending on lower-division students would have to be if it were true that it costs the same
amount to educate lower-division undergraduates in other sectors as it
does at community colleges.[38] Using the E&R expenditures per FTE student figure for community colleges in 2008, along with the other sectors' shares of all students who are lower-division undergraduates, we
have estimated the amount of E&R expenditures per FTE that must
have gone to advanced students in those other sectors *if* it is true that
the cost of educating lower-division undergraduates is equal across all
sectors.[39] The results of this exercise are shown in Table 8.

These estimates suggest that if it were true that the amount community
colleges spend on lower-division undergraduates is the same as the cost of
educating similar students in all of the other sectors, then the cost of educating advanced students would have to be only 1.4 times as high as the
cost of educating lower-division students at public master's universities,
twice as high at public research universities, but almost six times as high
at private research universities. The implication is that public master's
universities probably spend about as much on lower-division undergraduates, private research universities certainly spend more, and the other sectors probably spend somewhat more, but the exact difference is unclear.
These estimates of course ignore any impact on lower-division students of
studying in the same institution with more advanced students.[40]

We have repeated the exercise for state appropriations, focusing only
on public institutions. The results are shown in Table 9.

The estimates in Table 9 suggest that both public research and public
bachelor's institutions receive significantly higher appropriations than

TABLE 8
Hypothetical Education and Related Expenditures
per FTE Advanced Student, by Carnegie Sector, 2007–08
(in 2009 dollars)*

Carnegie Sector	E&R Expenditures per FTE Student at CCs	Residual E&R Expenditures per FTE Advanced Student	Implied Ratio of Advanced Student to Lower-Division UG E&R Expenditures per FTE
Public research	$9,481	$19,350	2.04
Public master's	$9,481	$13,288	1.4
Public bachelor's	$9,481	$21,148	2.23
Public associate's	$9,481	—	—
Private research	$9,481	$53,347	5.63
Private master's	$9,481	$19,478	2.05
Private bachelor's	$9,481	$30,131	3.18

*Residual E&R expenditures per FTE advanced student are calculated as follows:

$$\frac{\left(\begin{array}{c} ER\ Expenditures\ in \\ Specified\ Sector \end{array}\right) - \left(\begin{array}{c} ER\ Expenditures \\ per\ FTE\ CC\ Student \end{array}\right) \times \left(\begin{array}{c} FTE\ Lower\ Division\ UGs \\ in\ Specified\ Sector \end{array}\right)}{FTE\ Advanced\ Students\ in\ Specified\ Sector}$$

Source: The Delta Cost Project, American Institutes for Research; U.S. Department of Education, Institute of Education Sciences, National Center for Education Statistics, 2007–08 National Postsecondary Student Aid Study (NPSAS:08); calculations by the authors.

public associate's and public master's institutions for the education of lower-division undergraduates. The public bachelor's sector is relatively small, but it is focused on undergraduate students—and their appropriations would allow them to spend three times as much on advanced students as on lower-division students using the community college benchmark. Since 19 percent of the FTE students in public research universities are graduate students, the ratio of 2.91 does not imply as large a difference—but still suggests that there are more state funds available for lower-division undergraduates than is the case at community colleges. Public master's institutions—the most likely four-year alternative for community college students—are not so well funded and students enrolling in this sector do not appear to benefit from significantly more public funding than they would have in two-year institutions.

TABLE 9
Hypothetical State Appropriations per FTE Advanced Student,
by Carnegie Sector, 2007–08 (in 2009 dollars)*

Carnegie Sector	State and Local Appropriations per FTE Student at CCs	Residual Appropriations per FTE Advanced Student	Implied Ratio of Advanced Student to Lower-Division UG Appropriations per FTE
Public research	$4,209	$12,242	2.91
Public master's	$4,209	$7,895	1.88
Public bachelor's	$4,209	$12,611	3.00
Public associate's	$4,209	—	—

*Residual appropriation per FTE advanced student is calculated the same way that residual E&R expenditures per FTE advanced student are, the only difference being that appropriations are substituted for E&R expenditures in the equation.
Source: The Delta Cost Project, American Institutes for Research; U.S. Department of Education, Institute of Education Sciences, National Center for Education Statistics, 2007–08 National Postsecondary Student Aid Study (NPSAS:08); calculations by the authors.

WHAT ARE THE RELEVANT COMPARISONS FOR DETERMINING EQUITY?

Even if we could more accurately determine how much funding is devoted to educating students in different sectors, we would need a standard for determining how much *should* be spent. This is a normative question that cannot be settled with evidence alone. However, it may be possible to construct a framework from which to approach the issue analytically. We first pose questions about what would constitute equal funding levels and then ask what considerations might affect whether equal dollars translate into equal treatment for the different students enrolled in each sector of higher education.

Defining Equal Funding

Equality could be defined in terms of average dollars spent on educating students, in terms of average *public* funding per student, or in terms of subsidies. Student outcomes are obviously a function of total resources, not of public resources alone. But unequal access to private resources may not be a feasible public policy target in higher education.

It certainly seems unfair that a small number of students coming from disproportionately affluent backgrounds enroll in private institutions with unusually ample resources. It is hard to imagine that marginal dollars spent on these students at their unusually wealthy institutions yield benefits anywhere close to what might be the case if the resources were transferred to less-advantaged students enrolled in public institutions.

Despite the fact that a portion of the subsidies that wealthy private institutions receive comes from public funding, it is not easy develop practical suggestions for reallocating these resources. These colleges and universities could surely enroll more qualified, low-income students, but even significant increases would not touch the lives of the vast majority of disadvantaged students. Alternatively, the institutions could allocate a portion of their funds to scholarship aid for local students enrolled elsewhere or to the development of programs at cash-strapped institutions in the area. These unlikely developments could have a greater impact, but would not replace broad-based public policy changes involving the allocation of public resources.

Whether or not we can precisely define how much public funding is going to each community college student in a technical occupational training program or in a general studies program and to each lower-division undergraduate, upper-division undergraduate, and graduate student in a public master's or doctoral university studying engineering or philosophy, state and local governments must make decisions about the equitable and efficient allocation of resources.

If there were equal spending on community college and four-year public college students, community college students would have to get higher subsidies, since their relatively low tuition leaves a larger gap. Low tuition (in combination with ample state and federal grant aid) is central to the mission of community colleges. As the access point to postsecondary education and with predominantly low-income students, community colleges cannot reasonably raise tuition to levels approaching those of four-year institutions. Equal subsidies to the two groups will yield lower spending at two-year institutions.

The Case for Unequal Spending and Subsidies

One idea behind the community college system as a route to a viable system of mass postsecondary education is that these institutions can educate students more cheaply than four-year institutions can. They are teaching colleges with no significant research agenda and they can rely on faculty with lower-level credentials. Since teaching is the focus, faculty can teach more classes in this sector. Moreover, because they are generally not residential campuses, community colleges do not have to provide the array of amenities that are common in the four-year sector. While dormitories and dining halls may pay for themselves, other facilities and services for students whose lives are entirely on campus do not.

Community colleges are designed to make a part of the college experience easily accessible, both geographically and financially, to a broad range of students. Low prices and relatively low costs are parts of the strategy for making postsecondary education widely accessible. As discussed above, there are differences of opinion about whether spending on the education for lower-division undergraduates is really lower at community colleges. A very real question, however, is whether the characteristics of the student body and their academic and social needs require a different perspective on determining adequate resources.

It is almost certainly true that upper-division undergraduates—and, even more so, graduate students—require some resources not necessary for a solid beginning postsecondary education, particularly in the form of faculty skills and research context. But among beginning postsecondary students, there is an argument to be made that the typical community college student requires more resources than the typical lower-division student at, say, a public flagship university. Community college students generally come from lower-income backgrounds and have less academic preparation than their counterparts at four-year institutions.

Because of their socioeconomic and academic backgrounds, community college students are likely to need more remedial courses and to be more dependent on student support services in order to succeed in their studies than are lower-division students enrolled in four-year institutions. These circumstances compound the need for additional resources resulting from the fact that community college students are more likely to be engaged in vocational training in technical fields than are students at four-year institutions.

The low-income backgrounds of most community college students raise the question of whether equitable postsecondary funding requires compensation for inadequate access to resources earlier in life. The resources devoted to elementary and secondary education vary dramatically across school districts, but it is not possible to make general statements about the spending on low-income versus affluent students. In 2005–06, when average spending per student in the United States was $9,501, the average for high-poverty districts was $10,318—slightly lower than the $10,440 in low-poverty districts, but higher than the $8,731 to $9,070 in districts with intermediate levels of poverty.[41] In other words, generalizations about the resources devoted to the education of students before they arrive on college campuses are not likely to be accurate. That said, there is considerable evidence that the out-of-school resources, including enrichment spending by families in addition to community resources, are highly unequal and have grown more so over time.[42] It is hard to argue that "equal" treatment does not involve some level of compensatory funding.

The idea that low-income students need more resources in order to achieve outcomes approaching those of more affluent students has a long history in discussions of elementary and secondary school funding. There is widespread agreement that students for whom resources outside of the school environment are most limited and for whom other sources of enrichment are scarcest are most vulnerable to inadequately resourced schools.[43]

But there is no consensus that any amount of money would be able to close the gaps—or about how far additional money would go in narrowing those gaps. Even if there were a consensus with regard to K–12 education, it is not clear that the conclusions would transfer to postsecondary education.

The goals for high school outcomes are fairly standard across students. High school graduates should be college- and career-ready. Common core standards will make this consistency even clearer. But the range of outcomes sought by postsecondary students is much wider. Many community college students seek short-term certificates or other forms of job training. Some seek to transfer to four-year institutions. It is more expensive to train people for technical occupations than to teach a general liberal arts curriculum on the way to a bachelor's degree. But it is more expensive to have sophisticated science labs for advanced students than to teach people basic mathematics.

In addition to considering the equity implications of funding differences for public two-year and four-year students, it is important to examine efficiency considerations. What are the marginal benefits—to the individuals and to society—of additional investments in college students in different sectors? Could more resources devoted to community colleges improve credential attainment among students with disappointingly low completion rates? Should we focus resources on the students most likely to complete high-level STEM degrees or on those who will struggle to be productive members of the labor force if not provided with a stronger support system?

Aside from the rather obvious issue discussed above of the low marginal benefit of the extraordinary resources focused on a very small minority of students in the most elite institutions, these comparisons are difficult to make. It may be more constructive to focus on the adequacy of funding for community colleges and their students, rather than just on the distribution of the funding within higher education. Particularly in the current environment of diminished funding for education, it seems clear that at least at the federal level, there are public expenditures other than those on public flagship universities that would be better sources of increased revenues for community colleges. State budgets are more constrained, but there is no reason to focus only on the choices within the domain of education. The urgency of the problem is made more visible by cutbacks in course offerings and the resulting flight of students to the for-profit sector. A well-funded and strengthened two-year public college system is important for stemming the tide of students into expensive programs and institutions that too often leave them with unsustainable levels of debt, in addition to putting the nation's goal of a more educated, better-trained workforce into reach.

CONCLUSION

A definitive discussion of the adequacy of community college funding relative to other sectors of higher education would require a more nuanced data collection system allowing for the breakdown of expenditures across programs and years of study. Without these data, it is not possible to reliably compare the resources devoted to community college students to those devoted to similar students in other sectors. That said, some indicators point to problematic circumstances.

We cannot state definitively how educational expenditures per community college student compare to expenditures on lower-division students at four-year public colleges, although it appears that research universities do spend more educating their lower-division students. In any case, it is clear that expenditures have risen more rapidly at public research universities than in the sectors that educate more vulnerable student populations. Over the twenty years from 1989 to 2009, education and related expenditures per FTE student increased 23 percent in real terms at public research universities, 19 percent at public master's universities, 35 percent at public bachelor's colleges, and 17 percent at community colleges. There has been no increase at community colleges over the most recent decade.

State and local appropriations have actually been much more stable for community colleges than for public four-year colleges. Revenues per FTE community college student from this source were 3 percent higher in 2009 than in 1989, while there were declines of 20 percent at public research and 26 percent at public master's universities. Net tuition revenue has grown rapidly to compensate in these sectors, but that is not a viable strategy for community colleges.

It may be more constructive to focus on whether adequate resources are being devoted to the postsecondary education of disadvantaged students rather than on the comparison of the public funds—or the total amount of funding—devoted to educating students in different types of colleges. However, the lack of consensus on defining adequate funding in the K–12 education context provides a window into the even more difficult task in the realm of higher education. Because there is a consensus that students should not have to make a financial contribution to their own elementary/secondary education, only a total figure is needed—not a breakdown of that figure between the social and private responsibilities. In addition, the desired outcomes of postsecondary education are much more varied than those for K–12.

In other words, discussions of whether or not public funding of community colleges is adequate are likely to remain value-based debates for the foreseeable future. Improving the analytical framework for these debates is perhaps the most promising step for increasing the likelihood of moving public priorities in the direction of assuring educational opportunity. This effort requires several components:

1. *Better data.* National data should allow better separation of institutional expenditures on educating students at different levels of study (lower-level undergraduate, upper-level undergraduate, and graduate) and in different programs of study.
2. *Defining efficiency considerations.* Attempts to measure the social impact of increased levels of postsecondary educational attainment are widespread. Research on the differential impact of education at different types of institutions, in different programs, and for students with different characteristics and levels of preparation is less developed. Determining where society should put its marginal resources requires making hard choices among desirable goals and productive investments.

The public discourse currently reflects strong differences of opinion. On one hand, many people believe we are under-investing in at-risk students who have the potential to reap large benefits and make significant contributions if they are provided with strong postsecondary opportunities. Others contend that we are wasting resources by subsidizing students to enroll in colleges where they have little chance of earning credentials.

We need more evidence about the potential for alternative allocations of resources and alternative institutional structures to influence outcomes for at-risk students. We must also examine more carefully the return on investments in different types of students in different courses of study and in different types of institutions. The issue of at what stage of life additional investment is most productive is very relevant to this discussion.

3. *Defining equity considerations.* In addition to focusing on the loss of productivity and increased need for social support systems resulting from under-investment in the postsecondary education of disadvantaged students, we should strengthen the equity arguments underlying concerns about community college students and those enrolled in other institutions struggling to provide educational opportunity to lower-income, less-prepared students.

Pointing to the unsatisfactory outcomes of community college students would not be a sufficient argument, even if we could assert with confidence that more public resources are targeted at more privileged students. Better use of limited resources by both institutions and the students themselves surely has some potential to improve outcomes.

Perhaps the strongest equity argument for assuring that students from low-income backgrounds receive larger public subsidies than others do is the scarcity of private resources available to them. The question need not be just whether low-income students need more resources. There is a large and growing gap between the expenditures that middle- and upper-income families and communities devote to their young people and the resources available to those from low-income backgrounds. Compensating for these differences becomes more challenging the later in life the efforts are made.

There is broad consensus that our economy will require an increasing number of workers with postsecondary credentials, including many certificates and associate degrees. Establishing a secure middle-class standard of living without any postsecondary experience is very difficult. And many of the students who enroll in community colleges do not emerge with credentials. Additional resources, more effective use of those resources, and better guidance and support for students in both public two-year colleges and public four-year colleges serving disadvantaged and under-prepared students are surely necessary.

Whether or not funding formulas disadvantage community college students, it is clear that the shift away from a public priority on providing quality postsecondary educational opportunities to all who can benefit has a disproportionate impact on students without access to private resources to compensate for the loss of public investment. Students enrolling in community colleges and broad access four-year public institutions need better academic preparation and better-resourced institutions. Both their futures and the future of our economy and our society depend on our success in finding better ways to support their preparation for productive and financially secure lives.

NOTES

1. "About Community Colleges: Historical Information," American Association of Community Colleges, accessed August 4, 2012, http://www.aacc.nche.edu/aboutcc/history/Pages/default.aspx.

2. Truman Commission, *Higher Education for American Democracy*. Quoted in Philo Hutcheson, "The Truman Commission's Vision of the Future," *Thought and Action* (Fall 2007): 107–15.

3. Thomas D. Snyder and Sally A. Dillow, *Digest of Education Statistics 2011* (Washington, D.C.: U.S. Department of Education, National Center for Education Statistics, 2012), table 199.

4. Ibid., table 207.

5. Ibid., table 238.

6. U.S. Department of Education, Institute of Education Sciences, National Center for Education Statistics, Advance Release of Selected 2012 Digest Tables, table 201.5.

7. Snyder and Dillow, *Digest of Education Statistics 2011*, table 203.

8. U.S. Department of Education, Institute of Education Sciences, National Center for Education Statistics, 2007–08 National Postsecondary Student Aid Survey (NPSAS:08). Figures generated using the NCES's online Data Analysis System (DAS).

9. Ibid.

10. U.S. Department of Education, Institute of Education Sciences, National Center for Education Statistics, Integrated Postsecondary Education Data System (IPEDS): Completions Component. Figures generated using the NCES's online IPEDS Data Center.

11. Snyder and Dillow, *Digest of Education Statistics 2011*, table 296.

12. Anthony P. Carnevale, Stephen J. Rose, and Andrew R. Hanson, *Certificates: Gateway to Gainful Employment and College Degrees* (Washington, D.C.: Georgetown University Center on Education and the Workforce, 2012).

13. Don Hossler, Doug Shapiro, Afet Dundar, Mary Ziskin, Jin Chen, Desiree Zerquera, and Vasti Torres, *Transfer and Mobility: A National View of Pre-Degree Student Movement in Postsecondary Institutions* (Herndon, Va.: National Student Clearinghouse Research Center, 2012).

14. Kevin Dougherty, *The Contradictory College: The Conflicting Origins, Impacts, and Futures of the Community College* (Albany, N.Y.: State University of New York Press, 1994).

15. Synder and Dillow, *Digest of Education Statistics 2011*, table 226.

16. Sandy Baum and Jennifer Ma, "Trends in College Pricing 2012." The College Board, 2012.

17. Snyder and Dillow, *Digest of Education Statistics 2011*, table 226; Baum and Ma, "Trends in College Pricing 2012."

18. Michael Middaugh, Rosalina Graham, and Abdus Shait, *A Study of Higher Education Instructional Expenditures: The Delaware Study of Instructional Costs and Productivity*, NCES 2003-161 (Washington, D.C.: U.S. Department of Education, Institute of Education Sciences, National Center for Education Statistics, June 2003).

19. Richard M. Romano, Regina Losinger, and Tim Millard, "Measuring the Cost of a College Degree: A Case Study of a SUNY Community College," Cornell University ILR School, August 18, 2010.

20. David Breneman and Susan Nelson, *Financing Community Colleges: An Economic Perspective* (Washington, D.C.: The Brookings Institution, 1981); Estelle James, "Product Mix and Cost Disaggregation: A Reinterpretation of the Economics of Higher Education," *Journal of Human Resources* 13, no. 2 (Spring 1978): 157–86; June O'Neill, *Resource Use in Higher Education* (New York, N.Y.: Carnegie Commission on Higher Education, 1971); Cecilia E. Rouse, "Do Two-Year Colleges Increase Overall Educational Attainment? Evidence from the States," *Journal of Policy Analysis and Management* 17, no. 4 (1998): 595–620.

21. Richard Romano and Yenni M. Djajalaksana, "Using the Community College to Control College Costs: How Much Cheaper Is It?" Cornell University ILR School, 2010.

22. In the Delta Cost Project data, the "education share" of expenditures on academic support, institutional support, and operations and maintenance is calculated by taking the share of expenditures on instruction and student services in expenditures on instruction, student services, research, and public service, and then multiplying that fraction by spending on academic support, institutional support, and operations and maintenance.

23. The total revenue figure displayed in Table 4 and Figure 5 includes tuition revenue net of institutional grants, state and local appropriations, state and local grants and contracts, and federal revenue net of Pell grants. To facilitate comparisons

across institutional sectors, private gifts, investment returns, and endowment earnings, as well as revenues from auxiliary, hospitals, and other independent operations, have been omitted.

24. Revenues from auxiliary enterprises, hospitals, and other independent operations and from private gifts, grants, contracts, investment returns, and endowment earnings are excluded. The first group is approximately self-supporting and fluctuations in the second group make it difficult to evaluate the shares of other revenue sources when they are included.

25. Snyder and Dillow, *Digest of Education Statistics 2011*, table 261. Note that these ratios include both upper-division and lower-division undergraduates at public four-year institutions, where introductory level classes tend to be larger than upper-level classes.

26. Ibid., table 267.

27. Ibid., table 265.

28. Gordon Winston, "Subsidies, Hierarchy and Peers: The Awkward Economics of Higher Education," *Journal of Economic Perspectives* 12, no. 1 (Winter 1999): 13–36.

29. These universities were Harvard, Yale, Princeton, Stanford, MIT, Columbia, Northwestern, Penn, University of Chicago, Notre Dame, Duke, Emory, and Washington University.

30. National Association of College and University Business Officers, *NACUBO-Commonfund Endowment Study 2011* (Washington, D.C.: National Association of College and University Business Officers, 2011).

31. Baum and Ma, "Trends in College Pricing 2011," The College Board, 2011.

32. Jane G. Gravelle, "Tax Issues and University Endowments," Congressional Research Service, August 20, 2007.

33. Baum and Ma "Trends in College Pricing 2012."

34. National Association of College and University Business Officers and Commonfund Institute Study of Endowments, January 2012, available online at http://www.nacubo.org/Documents/research/2011_NCSE_Public_Tables_Avg_One_Three_Five_and_Ten_Year_Returns_Final_January_13_2012.pdf.

35. The nine are University of Michigan–Ann Arbor, University of Virginia–Charlottesville, University of Texas–Austin, University of Minnesota–Twin Cities, University of Pittsburgh, University of North Carolina–Chapel Hill, Ohio State University, University of Washington–Seattle, and Purdue University.

36. Office of Management and Budget, *Fiscal Year 2013 Analytical Perspectives: Budget of the U. S. Government* (Washington, D.C.: U.S. Government Printing Offices, 2012).

37. From here on, the term "advanced students" is used to refer to upper-division undergraduates, graduate students, and first-professional students.

38. Because we are unable to separate spending on graduate students from spending on undergraduates, we make the obviously inaccurate simplifying assumption that average spending on upper-division undergraduates is the same as spending on

graduate students. Since research universities have relatively more graduate students than master's universities, the ratios generated for that sector will over-estimate the amount they would be spending on advanced undergraduates.

39. According to data from the most recent National Postsecondary Student Aid Study (NPSAS:08), 92 percent of the students at community colleges were first- or second-year undergraduates in 2007–08. Assuming all of the students are in this category is not far from the reality.

40. It is also important to note that the ratio of graduate to undergraduate students differs markedly across sectors. We are unable to control for this difference because of the absence of data on the breakdown of upper- and lower-division undergraduates. In 2008–09, 44 percent of students in the private research universities were graduate students, compared to 30 percent in private master's, 23 percent in public research universities, and 15 percent in public master's universities (Delta Cost Project, www.deltacostproject.com).

41. Susan Aud et al., *The Condition of Education 2012*, NCES 2012-045 (Washington, D.C.: U.S. Department of Education, National Center for Education Statistics, May 2012).

42. Greg Duncan and Richard Murnane, "Introduction," in *Wither Opportunity*, ed. Greg Duncan and Richard Murnane (New York: Russell Sage Foundation and Chicago: Spencer Foundation, 2012).

43. Alan B. Krueger, Eric A. Hanushek, and Jennifer King Rice, The Class Size Debate (Washington, D.C.: Economic Policy Institute, 2012); Frederick Mosteller, "The Tennessee Study of Class Size in the Early School Grade" *The Future of Children* 5, no. 2 (Summer/Fall 1995).

School Integration and the Open Door Philosophy:
Rethinking the Economic and Racial Composition of Community Colleges

SARA GOLDRICK-RAB and PETER KINSLEY

There is longstanding and widespread interest in the relationship between the student composition of American schools and the outcomes they achieve, traceable to the famous finding of the Coleman Report that "the social composition of the student body is more highly related to achievement, independent of the student's own social background, than is any school factor."[1] African American and low-income students in particular appear to benefit academically from attending more-integrated schools.[2] While reasons for the seemingly positive influence of integration continue to be debated, segregation is nevertheless generally considered unacceptable in primary and secondary schooling, even as social class and race continues to segregate schools' surrounding neighborhoods.[3] Opportunities for learning, peer cultures, teacher quality and attitudes are all demonstrably constrained when students are confined to different spaces according to their family and cultural backgrounds. Thus, while the politics of desegregation are entrenched, efforts to decouple the composition of neighborhoods from the composition of schools continue, many decades after *Brown v. Board of Education*.[4]

We thank the Aspen Institute for providing data, and Derria Byrd and Sara Lazenby for providing research assistance.

The situation in postsecondary education is quite different. When it comes to the composition of colleges and universities, far less attention is paid to whether school-level integration by social class or race is *achieved*; rather the common focus is on *opportunity* for participation. In other words, the emphasis is typically placed on whether students from different backgrounds face similar chances of admission to institutions of higher education, rather than whether they experience and benefit from integrated learning environments once enrolled. This is likely partly attributable to societal norms treating K–12 schooling as a right and college as a privilege. It is also due to the widely accepted process of selective admissions shaping the college prospects of about one-fourth of American undergraduates.[5] But even at community colleges led with an "open door" philosophy, accessible by everyone in the neighborhood or district (irrespective, even, of high school graduation status), assessments of integration are rarely conducted.[6] Instead, the friendlier term "diversity" is used as a term of assessment, drawing attention to how *many* minority and/or low-income students are represented, rather than to the *relative* representation of groups strongly denoted by the term *integration*.[7]

If we accept the lessons from K–12 education that an integrated student body is preferable to a segregated student body when it comes to opportunities for learning, then we must confront the fact that *most of the nation's colleges and universities are highly segregated*.[8] Many states have perpetuated what expert Clifton Conrad calls "dual and unequal systems" of public higher education, in which historically black colleges and universities (HBCUs) remain under-resourced and threatened when compared with historically white colleges and universities.[9] Academic analyses of this problem tend to focus on the four-year sector, perhaps because access to the baccalaureate is a critical point for upward social mobility.[10] But the fact remains that in many parts of the United States, community colleges often enroll more Pell-eligible students and racial/ethnic minorities than many elite universities put together. For this, community colleges are typically praised for their diversity while elite universities are derided for a lack of diversity. Yet, in both cases, while the causes differ, *segregation* defines their student composition and corresponding opportunities for learning. The contribution of selective admissions policies and the use of test scores in creating this segregation is the subject of many other papers; in this one, we consider the dynamics of segregation among community colleges, where doors are wide open.

We focus on community colleges since they are the most affordable and accessible starting point in higher education, and thus the most common place for first-generation and racial/ethnic minority students to enter the postsecondary arena.[11] The research evidence pointing to the benefits of integration suggests that these are precisely the kinds of students who *most benefit* from participation in inclusive environments.[12] Growing up in segregated neighborhoods, children from disadvantaged backgrounds seem to excel when placed into K–12 schooling with children from more-advantaged backgrounds, and given that community college education is often essentially a continuation of K–12 schooling there is little reason to expect the effects would be differ in that setting. The problem is that the challenges facing K–12 schools in achieving integration are also faced by community colleges, but policymakers do far less to ensure that integration occurs. As inherently neighborhood institutions, community colleges are mission-driven to serve and represent their geographic regions. They fulfill this task: *we find that more than three-quarters of the variation in racial composition among community colleges is directly attributable to the racial composition of their surrounding geographic locales.* Given this tight relationship between housing and school integration, until neighborhoods are integrated, most community colleges will not be, absent affirmative steps.[13]

In this paper we document the extent of segregation in the nation's community colleges, and consider its relationship to neighborhood segregation. We further compare the organizational and institutional characteristics of community colleges enrolling segregated versus integrated student bodies, documenting many of the same sorts of resource disparities in the postsecondary setting that are well-documented in K–12. Then, we turn to lessons from analyses of documents written by community colleges (for the Aspen Prize for Community College Excellence) and interviews we conducted with community colleges that are more integrated than their surrounding counties would anticipate. Our results suggest that some communities are taking actions to diversify four-year institutions, steps that have the side effect of also better integrating community colleges. While recruiting more low-income and racial/ethnic minority high school graduates for four-year institutions rather than community colleges might reduce overall community college enrollment (desirable in some states due to crowding), it also effectively balances out the representation of students in both two-year and four-year settings, driving down the representation of poor and minority students at community colleges and increasing their representation at four-year public institutions. While such a strategy is not without substantial cost (for example, more financial aid is needed to finance a four-year education) and difficulty (for example, students must gain admission to four-year institutions), as well as other challenges (such as the geographic availability of four-year opportunities), it may result in more integrated and thus seemingly preferable learning environments in both spaces. Reforms in high schools, such as those aimed at improving the academic match between students and colleges, would seem likely to propel further moves in this direction.[14]

RESEARCH QUESTIONS

In order to consider the relationship between integration and the open-door policies of American community colleges, we ask the following questions: (1) What proportion of community colleges is economically and/or racially diverse? (2) How do the organizational characteristics of integrated community colleges compare to those that are segregated? (3) How well does geographic racial/ethnic and social class composition predict student body composition on those dimensions in community colleges? (4) How do the actual and expected student body composition (based on geography) at community colleges compare? How many community colleges appear out of sync with their geographic regions in a direction leaning toward more integration rather than segregation? (5) What factors seem to contribute to the ability of community colleges to achieve more integrated student bodies than expected?

METHODOLOGY

We examine these questions with national community college institutional data from the National Center for Education Statistics' 2010 Integrated Postsecondary Education Data System (IPEDS), merged with county-level data from the U.S. Census Bureau's 2010 American Community Survey. In addition, we supplement the analysis for the fifth question with data on a subset of community colleges from around the nation assembled by the Aspen Institute for its annual Prize for Community College Excellence competition, and a set of informal interviews conducted with institutions identified as outliers in the analysis for question four.[15] IPEDS data are limited for community colleges because IPEDS misses many students, but we use these data in the absence of anything better.

Addressing the first two research questions requires enumerating the number and characteristics of community colleges at various levels of economic and racial integration nationally, and then comparing college characteristics across these levels. Next, we address research question three by using OLS regression models to consider whether it is possible to explain levels of compositional diversity solely utilizing observable geographic characteristics of the communities in which the institutions are located.[16] These analyses provide some insight into the potential for community colleges to alter existing levels of segregation as a matter of institutional policy.

We then use the geographic models to predict the level of expected integration for each college, which we compare to the actual level of integration at the college. We subsequently sort community colleges into categories based on whether they are more or less integrated than expected. Setting aside any normative or value judgments, we consider whether greater integration seems to be achieved through an overrepresentation of advantaged (that is, middle income and/or white) students, an overrepresentation of disadvantaged students, or an underrepresentation of disadvantaged students. In each case, representation is a relative term, and comparisons are made to communities. Finally, we leverage qualitative data from the Aspen Prize applications along with data from informal interviews conducted with specific "outlier" colleges to examine how these colleges seem to differ from the others in terms of how they define student success, use data, construct policies and practices, and create diversity.[17]

DEFINING INTEGRATION

For many decades, policymakers, lawyers, practitioners, educators, and parents have fought over what constitutes an "integrated" school. While many can agree that integration implies a "balance" of some kind, the inherent relativity of the term and its political connotations make it hard to arrive at a clear and uncontroversial definition. Yet definitions are critical for the creation of comparisons, and thus we undertake them here in the spirit of knowingly quantifying the possibly unquantifiable— for pragmatic reasons, if nothing else.

A college's level of economic integration is based on the proportion of first-time, full-time, degree-seeking students receiving a Pell Grant. This is the best available measure and yet is a highly flawed proxy for low-income representation at an institution because it is affected by Free Application for Federal Student Aid (FAFSA) completion rates, inconsistent methods used by community colleges to determine first-time and degree-seeking students, and the fact that only a fraction of community college students enroll full-time.[18] More straightforward is a college's level of racial integration which we base on the proportion of racial or ethnic minority students in the entire student body.[19]

A simple assessment of integration using the *average* characteristics of all community colleges suggests that 52 percent of their students receive Pell, and 33 percent are racial/ethnic minorities (Table 1). However, these averages conceal considerable meaningful variation *among* institutions. To describe that range and how it relates to segregation and integration, we examined prior studies in K–12 education and higher education to determine cut-points that could be used to determine whether a given level of racial and low-income enrollment could be said to be effectively segregated or integrated. Unfortunately, we found little guidance in the higher education literature, which has traditionally approached the issue of college racial profile through comparisons of historically black institutions (HBI) and predominately white institutions (PWI)—essentially, whether or not a college includes majority non-Hispanic white students. Studies of racial integration in K–12, on the other hand, typically examine the equitable distribution of minority populations within school districts—an approach with limited applicability to community colleges due to their more sparse geographic distribution and fundamentally different governance structures. After trying several strategies for breaking down the school-level proportions into groups, including various cut points relative to the national means of our measures, we settled on a relatively straightforward approach: dividing the national distributions of proportion Pell and minority enrollment into quartiles. In the end, we feel that this approach does the best job of balancing statistical power, face validity, and ease of data interpretation. It also offers the benefit of remaining grounded in how community colleges actually perform regarding their enrollment of minority and low-income students while also allowing for more subjective judgments of integration at the national level.

Using this approach, the data suggest that about *half of the nation's community colleges are economically integrated*, with the representation of Pell recipients at those colleges ranging between 47 percent and 58 percent (Table 1, quartiles 2 and 3). One-fourth of community colleges are economically elite (in relative terms), with advantaged students (those not receiving Pell) constituting 68 percent of the student body. Fully 25 percent of community colleges are predominantly poor, with nearly three in four students receiving the Pell Grant.

TABLE 1
Community College Characteristics by Proportion Pell Receipt Among First-Time, Full-Time Students

	Total		Quartile 1		Quartile 2		Quartile 3		Quartile 4		Comparison	
	Mean	SD	Mean	SD	Mean	SD	Mean	SD	Mean	SD	F-value	Sig.
N	(966)		(250)		(257)		(237)		(222)			
Enrollment Composition (%)												
Total enrollment	7461.96	7401.38	10584.37	8650.14	7973.22	7887.03	6180.47	5801.61	4721.92	5124.35	30.28	***
Pell (first-time, full-time)	51.89	15.85	32.06	7.39	47.36	3.09	57.93	3.22	73.02	7.57	2176.00	***
Minority (±)	32.53	22.67	30.17	15.91	28.80	19.46	28.41	21.63	43.93	29.13	26.52	***
Female	58.08	7.47	55.79	6.34	56.63	8.32	58.68	6.26	61.69	7.38	31.57	***
Full-time	45.31	14.02	40.27	12.65	43.84	13.49	47.09	13.48	50.77	14.43	26.10	***
Full-time, first-time degree seeking	12.77	7.17	10.95	7.17	12.58	7.49	13.49	6.23	14.28	7.33	9.73	***
Cost of Attendance ($)												
Total cost of attendance	15116.15	3178.21	15906.98	3183.11	15076.48	3261.27	15016.52	2669.81	14387.42	3395.46	9.12	***
Instructional Offerings (%)												
Occupational	97.31	16.19	98.00	14.03	98.05	13.84	97.05	16.97	95.95	19.77	0.88	
Academic	96.58	18.17	99.20	8.93	97.28	16.31	98.31	12.91	90.99	28.70	9.84	***
Distance learning	98.03	13.89	97.60	15.34	98.44	12.40	100.00	0.00	95.95	19.77	3.44	**
Weekend/evening programs	61.80	48.61	66.80	47.19	59.92	49.10	59.92	49.11	60.36	49.03	1.19	
Remedial services	99.48	7.18	99.20	8.93	99.61	6.24	100.00	0.00	99.10	9.47	0.78	

(continued)

TABLE 1
Community College Characteristics by Proportion Pell Receipt Among First-Time, Full-Time Students (continued)

	Total		Quartile 1		Quartile 2		Quartile 3		Quartile 4		Comparison	
	Mean	SD	Mean	SD	Mean	SD	Mean	SD	Mean	SD	F-value	Sig.
Student Services (%)												
Academic/career counseling	99.79	4.55	100.00	0.00	100.00	0.00	99.58	6.50	99.55	6.71	0.74	
Student employment assistance	92.24	26.77	94.80	22.25	94.94	21.96	90.72	29.08	87.84	32.76	3.93	**
On-campus day care	51.86	49.99	64.40	47.98	55.25	49.82	46.84	50.01	39.19	48.93	11.56	***
On-campus housing	23.29	42.29	15.20	35.97	25.29	43.55	31.65	46.61	21.17	40.94	6.62	***
Meal plan	20.08	40.08	13.20	33.92	22.18	41.63	26.58	44.27	18.47	38.89	4.95	***
Financial Aid Receipt (first-time, full-time students)												
Average pell amount	4266.79	513.58	4134.56	543.25	4168.59	417.18	4342.29	478.12	4448.76	550.59	20.87	***
Percent receiving federal loans	23.56	21.40	15.88	15.68	27.45	21.36	29.76	21.86	21.10	23.50	22.60	***
Average amount of federal loan	4428.73	1202.51	4295.25	1048.45	4483.56	1175.45	4621.29	1192.16	4279.59	1434.70	3.61	**
Staffing												
Student-to-faculty ratio	21.39	6.60	22.05	6.50	21.47	7.26	21.24	5.49	20.68	6.95	1.74	
Student to administrative/managerial ratio	234.13	231.78	253.92	207.32	243.13	233.67	215.90	175.91	220.90	297.98	1.47	
Student to support staff ratio	186.67	671.32	348.12	1193.37	186.43	483.30	121.28	274.27	82.01	94.90	7.26	***
Average nine-month instructional staff salary ($)	57021.55	14048.71	65346.51	15460.31	57243.54	12684.75	54015.52	12234.19	50599.76	10795.43	56.75	***
All staff percent minority (‡)	27.31	21.16	29.16	19.19	23.62	19.46	22.23	17.43	34.60	26.71	6.28	***

Instructional staff percent minority (‡)	23.74	20.33	25.98	20.13	20.19	17.03	19.31	16.83	29.59	25.52	5.12	***
Revenues												
Core revenues ($ million)	53.70	50.25	72.71	58.89	56.43	50.89	45.18	39.02	38.24	41.95	22.90	***
Revenues from tuition and fees per FTE ($)	1939.45	1191.31	2146.09	1331.70	2130.18	1169.92	1876.68	1007.82	1552.69	1132.21	13.20	***
Tuition and fees as percent of core revenues	16.92	10.13	19.07	11.74	18.18	9.22	16.92	8.97	13.05	9.30	16.67	***
Revenues from state appropriations per FTE ($)	3217.80	1949.61	3093.63	2205.12	3234.98	1815.43	3127.03	1665.99	3434.63	2065.32	1.43	
State appropriations as percent of core revenues	27.57	13.10	26.65	14.33	27.82	12.92	27.19	11.88	28.74	13.09	1.10	
Revenues from local appropriations per FTE ($)	1649.12	3264.91	2305.86	2526.97	2039.04	5174.98	1292.14	2157.03	836.96	1347.50	10.37	***
Local appropriations as percent of core revenues	12.95	15.65	19.96	18.54	13.90	15.61	10.11	13.17	6.97	10.64	33.42	***
Expenditures												
Core expenses ($ million)	48.77	46.01	66.37	54.44	51.31	45.74	40.31	34.52	35.03	39.79	23.23	***
Instruction expenses per FTE ($)	4763.31	2020.16	4891.47	2010.06	5020.94	2631.74	4465.30	1528.80	4637.55	1592.00	3.76	**
Instruction expenses as a percent of total core	44.56	8.80	46.72	8.77	45.63	9.22	43.46	7.43	42.08	8.95	13.93	***
Academic support expenses per FTE ($)	955.47	839.29	1002.10	652.58	1010.32	1198.88	851.66	518.08	949.83	790.54	1.83	
Academic support expenses as percent of total	8.74	4.55	9.58	5.06	8.81	4.37	8.22	3.96	8.27	4.64	4.74	***

(continued)

TABLE 1
Community College Characteristics by Proportion Pell Receipt Among First-Time, Full-Time Students (continued)

	Total		Quartile 1		Quartile 2		Quartile 3		Quartile 4		Comparison	
	Mean	SD	Mean	SD	Mean	SD	Mean	SD	Mean	SD	F-value	Sig.
Student support expenses per FTE ($)	1221.84	918.00	1156.41	596.68	1289.05	1134.62	1168.28	856.39	1274.64	993.85	1.40	
Student support expenses as percent of total core	11.10	5.20	10.90	3.62	11.22	4.83	11.23	6.45	11.05	5.62	0.22	
Institutional support expenses per FTE ($)	1776.52	1317.07	1875.22	1316.41	1783.48	1669.03	1640.11	969.61	1802.35	1164.49	1.34	
Institutional support expenses as percent of core	15.84	6.04	16.90	6.95	15.43	5.25	15.48	6.11	15.50	5.61	3.48	**

Notes: Q1 = 0–41 percent Pell receipt; Q2 = 42–52 percent Pell receipt; Q3 = 53–63 percent Pell receipt; Q4 = 64–100 percent Pell receipt. One-way ANOVA test for mean differences; ** .05; *** .01.

‡ n=374

± Students of unknown race removed from total enrollment when calculating minority percentages

Source: U.S. Department of Education, Institute of Education Sciences, National Center for Education Statistics, Integrated Postsecondary Education Data System (IPEDS) 2010.

The story with regard to race/ethnicity is even more troubling. Just 25 *percent of community colleges approach racial integration,* with the representation of racial/ethnic minorities averaging 36.5 percent (Table 2, quartile 3). Another quarter of all community colleges are comprised of predominantly white students, with minorities constituting just 8 percent of the student body. Another 25 percent are predominantly minority, where 65 percent of students at the colleges are racial/ethnic minorities.[20] The remaining quarter is in-between—not integrated, yet not strongly segregated either.

CHARACTERISTICS OF INTEGRATED COMMUNITY COLLEGES

How do integrated and segregated community colleges differ from one another? Tables 1 and 2 present the relevant comparisons, and we first focus primarily on the differences between quartiles 2 and 3 versus 1 and 4 with regard to economic integration (Table 1), and then quartile 3 versus all others with regard to racial integration (Table 2).[21]

More economically and racially integrated institutions tend to be of moderate size—between 6,000 and 9,000 students—while predominantly poor institutions are smaller, and predominantly minority institutions are notably larger (and urban).

It is fairly uncommon for community colleges to be compositionally integrated on multiple dimensions. Apart from those with the most affluent student bodies, community colleges exhibit racial integration at levels close to the national average (about one-third minority enrollment). Similarly, only community colleges with the highest proportions of minority students (quartile 4) have rates of Pell receipt notably higher than the national average (about one-half Pell enrollment). Economically and/or racially integrated institutions are also somewhat more integrated in terms of gender when compared to institutions with the highest proportions of minority or low-income students (this means they have a smaller fraction of women, who tend to dominate colleges and universities).

Economically integrated community colleges tend to have more full-time students compared to institutions enrolling more economically advantaged students. They are also more likely to have academic offerings, offer student employment assistance, on-campus childcare, and/or on-campus housing and meals plans, compared to institutions that are segregated because of an overrepresentation of Pell recipients.

TABLE 2
National Community College Characteristics by Proportion Racial Minority/Hispanic Enrollment

	Total		Quartile 1		Quartile 2		Quartile 3		Quartile 4		Comparison	
	Mean	SD	Mean	SD	Mean	SD	Mean	SD	Mean	SD	F-value	Sig.
N	(966)		(242)		(241)		(242)		(241)			
Enrollment Composition (%)												
Total enrollment	7461.96	7401.38	4144.74	2983.30	7345.12	5997.95	8743.52	8805.39	9622.88	8946.40	27.60	***
Pell (first-time, full-time)	51.89	15.85	54.13	12.20	45.75	13.60	48.47	16.53	59.21	17.12	38.62	***
Minority	32.53	22.67	8.38	3.45	20.71	4.21	36.52	5.19	64.62	15.20	1982.44	***
Female	58.08	7.47	57.43	7.56	57.44	6.97	57.97	7.26	59.48	7.91	4.09	***
Full-time	45.31	14.02	49.52	12.71	45.77	12.68	44.00	13.52	41.93	15.88	13.23	***
Full-time, first-time degree seeking	12.77	7.17	14.64	6.86	13.18	7.33	12.27	7.20	10.99	6.82	11.47	***
Cost of Attendance ($)												
Total cost of attendance	15116.15	3178.21	14773.29	3339.25	15050.09	3275.21	15346.85	3136.74	15288.19	2940.88	1.60	
Instructional Offerings (%)												
Occupational	97.31	16.19	97.93	14.25	99.17	9.09	96.28	18.96	95.85	19.98	2.17	
Academic	96.58	18.17	99.59	6.43	97.51	15.61	94.63	22.59	94.61	22.64	4.34	***
Distance learning	98.03	13.89	99.17	9.07	97.93	14.28	98.35	12.78	96.68	17.95	1.35	
Weekend/evening programs	61.80	48.61	59.09	49.27	60.58	48.97	57.02	49.61	70.54	45.68	3.71	**
Remedial services	99.48	7.18	99.59	6.43	99.59	6.44	99.59	6.43	99.17	9.09	0.20	

Student Services (%)

Academic/career counseling	99.79	4.55	100.00	0.00	99.59	6.44	99.59	6.43	100.00	0.00	0.67
Student employment assistance	92.24	26.77	92.15	26.95	94.61	22.64	91.32	28.21	90.87	28.86	0.93
On-campus day care	51.86	49.99	43.80	49.72	56.43	49.69	46.69	49.99	60.58	48.97	6.17 ***
On-campus housing	23.29	42.29	29.34	45.63	27.80	44.89	21.49	41.16	14.52	35.31	6.26 ***
Meal plan	20.08	40.08	24.79	43.27	24.07	42.84	18.60	38.99	12.86	33.55	4.68 ***
Financial Aid Receipt (first-time, full-time students)											
Average pell amount	4266.79	513.58	4196.60	468.41	4178.40	530.39	4329.50	525.75	4362.67	505.33	8.06 ***
Percent receiving federal loans	23.56	21.40	37.96	21.45	27.43	20.77	18.33	18.21	10.49	13.82	95.80 ***
Average amount of federal loan	4428.73	1202.51	4473.26	1194.42	4491.79	1100.52	4400.86	1228.66	4324.05	1302.32	0.77
Staffing											
Student-to-faculty ratio	21.39	6.60	19.25	5.35	20.73	4.90	21.84	5.71	23.73	8.89	21.00 ***
Student to administrative/managerial ratio	234.13	231.78	206.87	219.45	208.96	180.67	244.30	196.56	276.49	304.72	4.96 ***
Student to support staff ratio	186.67	671.32	84.63	112.61	123.28	282.04	245.72	1033.96	294.00	786.15	5.22 ***
Average nine-month instructional staff salary ($)	57021.55	14048.71	52843.04	8660.73	57382.04	12415.76	57333.12	15674.54	60526.71	16934.64	12.64 ***
All staff percent minority (‡)	27.31	21.16	10.14	14.43	16.43	15.77	25.30	12.32	49.06	16.88	124.12 ***
Instructional staff percent minority (‡)	23.74	20.33	11.01	18.47	14.83	16.25	21.25	13.28	41.49	17.94	66.14 ***

(continued)

TABLE 2
National Community College Characteristics by Proportion Racial Minority/Hispanic Enrollment (continued)

	Total (n = 983)		Quartile 1		Quartile 2		Quartile 3		Quartile 4		Comparison	
	Mean	SD	Mean	SD	Mean	SD	Mean	SD	Mean	SD	F-value	Sig.
Revenues												
Core revenues ($ million)	53.70	50.25	32.28	21.39	54.14	42.80	61.14	59.65	67.32	59.88	23.92	***
Revenues from tuition and fees per FTE ($)	1939.45	1191.31	2354.24	1264.31	2319.44	1216.46	1743.48	978.27	1341.46	972.47	45.98	***
Tuition and fees as percent of core revenues	16.92	10.13	19.74	9.78	20.54	10.62	16.10	9.42	11.30	7.83	47.78	***
Revenues from state appropriations per FTE ($)	3217.80	1949.61	3311.88	1721.56	3076.44	1942.54	3289.64	2073.53	3192.23	2044.34	0.73	
State appropriations as percent of core revenues	27.57	13.10	27.43	11.48	26.02	13.15	28.95	13.08	27.88	14.43	2.08	
Revenues from local appropriations per FTE ($)	1649.12	3264.91	1485.53	2572.31	1719.68	2471.12	1586.64	2115.89	1805.84	5057.69	0.45	
Local appropriations as percent of core revenues	12.95	15.65	10.64	14.80	13.74	16.40	13.50	16.53	13.91	14.62	2.37	
Expenditures												
Core expenses ($ million)	48.77	46.01	29.55	19.96	48.79	38.44	55.65	54.77	61.15	55.20	23.20	***
Instruction expenses per FTE ($)	4763.31	2020.16	4988.51	1909.22	4843.49	1610.90	4597.43	1665.64	4624.49	2694.75	2.05	
Instruction expenses as a percent of total core	44.56	8.80	44.72	9.09	46.24	8.49	45.69	8.20	41.60	8.72	13.92	***

Academic support expenses per FTE ($)	955.47	839.29	928.50	595.07	955.79	582.01	862.97	484.15	1075.00	1370.19	2.71 **
Academic support expenses as percent of total	8.74	4.55	8.40	4.69	9.10	4.68	8.60	3.97	8.86	4.83	1.10
Student support expenses per FTE ($)	1221.84	918.00	1182.77	730.92	1232.72	722.57	1109.25	719.66	1363.07	1331.93	3.29 ***
Student support expenses as percent of total core	11.10	5.20	10.67	5.92	11.40	4.57	10.72	4.35	11.63	5.72	2.10
Institutional support expenses per FTE ($)	1776.52	1317.07	1911.29	1140.29	1707.06	868.59	1621.14	947.21	1867.24	1989.04	2.58
Institutional support expenses as percent of core	15.84	6.04	16.77	7.34	15.90	5.04	15.66	5.58	15.02	5.87	3.49 **

‡ n=374

Notes: Minority includes: African American, Hispanic, Native American, Pacific Islander, Mixed Race/Ethnicity. Students of unknown race removed from total when calculating minority quartiles. Q1 = 2–14 percent minority; Q2 = 14–28 percent minority; Q3 = 28–46 percent minority; Q4: 46–100 percent minority. One-way ANOVA test for mean differences; ** .05; *** .01.

Source: U.S. Department of Education, Institute of Education Sciences, National Center for Education Statistics, Integrated Postsecondary Education Data System (IPEDS) 2010.

However, in other regards, economically integrated community colleges appear to have fewer resources than predominantly poor institutions—for example, their student-to-support staff ratios are notably higher. On the other hand, they tend to have higher staff salaries and more core revenue, especially from local appropriations (though much lower than at institutions with fewer Pell recipients).

Compared to predominantly minority serving community colleges, racially integrated community colleges (Table 2, quartiles 4 versus 3) have higher percentages of full-time, first-time degree-seeking students, are more likely to offer on-campus housing and meal plans, and are less likely to offer on-campus daycare. Far more of their students have federal loans. There are far fewer students per faculty member, administrative, and support staff, but the average staff salary is lower. They have fewer external sources of revenue and rely more on tuition. They have fewer expenses and devote a larger fraction of the core budget to instruction.

Compared to predominantly white institutions (quartiles 1 versus 3), racially integrated colleges have fewer full-time students, are less likely to have academic offerings, are more likely to offer daycare but less likely to offer on-campus housing and meal plans, and have far fewer resources per student. In other words, the more minority students a college enrolls, the fewer organizational advantages it enjoys.

Turning next to comparisons among segregated institutions, we find sharp differences between those that are heavily affluent and/or non-Hispanic white, compared to those that enroll predominantly poor and/or racial-ethnic minority students. Community colleges serving overwhelmingly minority populations are much larger than those serving largely non-Hispanic white students (average total enrollment of 9,623 versus 4,145). Compared to staff at predominantly white institutions, staff members at predominately minority institutions—particularly instructional staff—are far more likely to be from minority backgrounds themselves.[22] Community colleges with a high proportion of minority students also have much higher ratios of students to faculty, staff, and administrators. For example, there are on average 85 students per support staff member at predominantly white community colleges, compared with 294 students per support staff member at predominantly minority community colleges. However, the opposite is true when it comes to economic segregation: institutions that are wealthier, with fewer Pell recipients, have much larger student-to-staff ratios, compared to those with very high percentages of Pell recipients.

Even though predominately minority institutions are larger and thus generate more revenue, the amount of per-FTE revenue from tuition and fees generated at predominately white institutions is nearly double that of the revenue generated per FTE at minority-serving community colleges. Moreover, institutions serving wealthier students gain far more money from local appropriations than those serving large proportions of Pell recipients, which is unsurprising given the relative wealth of their communities. That said, the data available suggest that both types of institutions allocate their revenue in similar ways.

GEOGRAPHIC INTEGRATION AND COMMUNITY COLLEGE INTEGRATION: TIGHTLY LINKED

To what degree does the level of integration or segregation at community colleges reflect geographic constraints? In other words, given that theory and research suggests advantages to educating students in more integrated settings, it is useful to consider what generates such integration.

To examine this, we model the relationships between county-level measures of population composition and measures of community college student composition. The analytic strategy utilizes multivariate regression models with ordinary least squares as the estimator. To adjust for unobserved factors at the state level such as policies that may influence the practices of all community colleges in the state regarding enrollment of minority and/or low-income students, we run all of our models using state fixed effects. To aid in interpretation of our results we report the standardized coefficient for each of our predictors—interpreted as the expected standard deviation change in the outcome resulting from a standard deviation increase in the predictor—which allows for a direct comparison of effect sizes across all variables in the model.

Table 3 presents the results of two models in which we estimate the proportion of first-time, full-time Pell enrollment at community colleges, first using county-level measures of integration, and then controlling for urbanicity and a select group of institutional characteristics—cost, size, and HBCU or Native American tribal affiliation. The results indicate that more than half (56 percent) of the variation in the representation of Pell recipients among community colleges is attributable to this limited set of factors. In fact, most of the variation in community colleges' economic composition can be predicted based solely on knowing the percent of low-income, minority, and female adults in their counties, along with the unemployment rate.

TABLE 3
OLS Regression Models Predicting Proportion
First-Time, Full-Time Pell Enrollment

	Model 1			Model 2		
	Beta	R.S.E.	Sig.	Beta	R.S.E.	Sig.
County-Level						
Percent low-income	0.512	0.038	***	0.459	0.043	***
Percent minority	−0.003	0.038		−0.022	0.043	
Percent female	0.005	0.034		0.029	0.031	
Unemployment rate	0.107	0.039	***	0.107	0.035	***
Urbanicity						
Rural-serving medium area				−0.158	0.085	
Rural-serving large area				−0.291	0.104	***
Suburban				−0.335	0.107	***
Urban				0.056	0.118	
Institution-Level						
Total cost of attendance				0.018	0.032	
Total enrollment				−0.098	0.031	***
HBCU or tribal affiliation				0.877	0.215	***
Constant	−0.690	0.084	***	−0.405	0.118	***
N	966			945		
R-Squared	0.507			0.562		

Notes: Standardized coefficients; robust standard errors; state fixed effects to adjust for state-level unobservable factors. Rural-serving small area is urbanicity reference.
.05; *.01

Geography plays an even stronger role with regard to the racial composition of community colleges. Table 4 shows that fully 81 percent of variation in racial composition among students at community colleges is predicted by the percent of low-income, minority, and female adults in their surrounding counties, coupled with the unemployment rate. Knowing some additional institutional information helps explain the variation in composition a bit more, but it is clear that the degree to which racial/ethnic minority students are represented at community colleges depends

TABLE 4
OLS Regression Models Predicting Proportion Minority Enrollment

	Model 1			Model 2		
	Beta	R.S.E.	Sig.	Beta	R.S.E.	Sig.
County-Level						
Percent low-income	−0.088	0.026	***	−0.089	0.027	***
Percent minority	0.903	0.027	***	0.830	0.028	***
Percent female	−0.020	0.022		0.005	0.018	
Unemployment rate	0.019	0.025		0.010	0.024	
Urbanicity						
Rural-serving medium area				−0.087	0.044	**
Rural-serving large area				−0.108	0.055	
Suburban				−0.056	0.061	
Urban				0.121	0.069	
Institution-Level						
Total cost of attendance				−0.009	0.018	
Total enrollment				−0.006	0.019	
HBCU or tribal affiliation				1.051	0.164	***
Constant	−0.021	0.050		0.072	0.064	
N	966			945		
R-Squared	0.810			0.849		

Notes: Standardized coefficients; robust standard errors; state fixed effects to adjust for state-level unobservable factors. Rural-serving small area is urbanicity reference.
.05; *.01

quite substantially on whether they live in the surrounding county. In other words, county-level segregation is a very strong predictor of community college segregation.

Given the demonstrably strong relationship between county and community college demographics, few community colleges are unexpectedly integrated. To capture the degree to which unexpected integration does occur, we conduct a residual value analysis. Using the full regression models in Tables 5 and 6 we calculate the predicted enrollment of Pell and minority students at each college and then subtracted those values

TABLE 5
Residual Analysis of Pell Grant Enrollment

	N	Mean	SD	Min	Max
A. Pell Residual Summary Statistics by Group					
Group 1	132	−16.92	5.99	−39.72	−10.59
Group 2	341	−4.53	2.99	−10.44	0.00
Group 3	345	4.80	2.89	0.04	10.44
Group 4	127	16.70	6.06	10.49	48.16
Total	945				
B. Percent Pell Distribution Across Residual Groups					
Group 1	132	36.20	13.81	5.00	74.00
Group 2	341	46.35	12.33	19.00	98.00
Group 3	345	57.11	11.92	26.00	86.00
Group 4	127	69.56	12.06	44.00	100.00
Total	945				

Notes: Group 1: Residual value more than 1 SD below the mean; Group 2: Residual value within 1 SD below the mean; Group 3: Residual value within 1 SD above the mean; Group 4: Residual value more than 1 SD above the mean.

from the achieved enrollment proportions to arrive at a residual value. A negative residual indicates that a college is enrolling fewer poor or minority students than geography would predict, while a positive value indicates the opposite. Greater integration could be achieved from either positive or negative residuals; there is no inherently preferred value from a normative perspective, but rather would depend on where a college falls in terms of its predicted level of segregation. We distinguish between four groups based on their degree of deviance from the expected level of integration: (1) substantial deviance (>1 standard deviation below the mean) tilting toward the integration of more advantaged students, (2) slight deviance (<1 SD below the mean) tilting toward the integration of more advantaged students, (3) slight deviance tilting toward integration of more disadvantaged students, and (4) substantial deviance tilting toward integration of more disadvantaged students.

As noted earlier, about half of the nation's community college enroll balanced student bodies with approximately equal numbers of Pell recipients and non-recipients (Table 1). These analyses suggest that

TABLE 6
Residual Analysis of Racial/Ethnic Minority Enrollment

	Obs	Mean	SD	Min	Max
A. Pell Residual Summary Statistics by Group					
Group 1	91	−16.17	6.12	−34.79	−9.06
Group 2	456	−2.85	2.51	−9.02	0.67
Group 3	276	4.35	2.75	0.71	10.37
Group 4	122	18.16	8.50	10.48	50.97
Total	945				
B. Percent Minority Across Residual Groups					
Group 1	91	33.17	16.25	4.45	85.73
Group 2	456	23.20	17.78	1.71	100.00
Group 3	276	35.32	20.28	3.79	94.90
Group 4	122	62.79	21.31	17.91	98.28
Total	945				

Notes: Group 1: residual value more than 1 SD below the mean; Group 2: residual value within 1 SD below the mean; Group 3: residual value within 1 SD above the mean; Group 4: residual value more than 1 SD above the mean.

some of this is due to about 27 percent of community colleges enrolling far more or less Pell recipients than geography would dictate (Table 5, Panel A). Approximately half of those colleges enroll more (13 percent), and half enroll less (14 percent). But there is less deviation at community colleges with regard to enrollment of race/ethnic minority students, and correspondingly a lower degree of racial integration. Just 23 percent of community colleges have a racial/ethnic composition out of step with their geography. Thirteen percent have an over-segregation of minority students in their schools, while 10 percent of institutions enroll a less-segregated student body than geography alone would predict. (Table 6, Panel B).

INTEGRATION: HAPPENSTANCE OR ACHIEVED?

Are greater-than-expected levels of integration in community college the result of a happy coincidence or intentional action? This is a critical question that is clearly difficult to answer. However, next we leverage

the limited amount of qualitative data we have available to try and provide some insights.

In writing applications for the national Aspen Prize for community
colleges, institutions attempt to put their best foot forward and describe
their approaches to serving students. A close textual analysis of their
applications, focused on the "outlier" institutions whose college composition deviates from the geographic norm, suggests that community
college administrators are conscious of the composition of their student bodies, and in particular are conscious when their composition is
unusual. Institutions with disproportionate numbers of minority and/
or low-income students are more likely to explicitly report using quantitative measures to assess institutional diversity, perhaps because they
are more conscious of that attribute and may be getting attention for
it, or perhaps are concerned about it. For example, one college notes
that "directors, chairs, and other staff use special Institutional Research
studies to plan and improve programs: such as high school draw by
race/ethnicity; placement test results by entry status, race/ethnicity, and
high school; and retention rates by campus, gender, and race/ethnicity."
These schools are also more likely than non-outlier institutions to mention having external partnerships specifically aimed at underrepresented
populations. The discourse used by community colleges in their applications to Aspen also varies in relation to the actual versus expected level
of integration among students at their schools. Community colleges that
enrolled somewhat more Pell recipients than their surrounding area
would predict tend to emphasize the greater representation of economically disadvantaged and first-generation students, highlighting that attribute for readers. For example, one such college administrator notes that
his institution "prizes" the "diversity" of its students.

By contrast, colleges disproportionately enrolling advantaged students say far less in their applications about the composition of their
institutions and do not describe any particular programs addressing
composition. But in many cases these institutions are nonetheless more
integrated than other community colleges, even when not explicitly
emphasizing that fact.

While such observations are useful for thinking about the potential
role of specific practices and attitudes in creating integrated student bodies, we went a step further and undertook informal phone interviews
with fourteen community colleges where the enrollment of Pell recipients
and racial/ethnic minority students in our data was more integrated or
balanced than predicted by geography. Bringing this observation to the

attention of college staff, we posed the question: "What might contribute to this integration?" After frequently having to define the term *integration*, about three-quarters of the administrators provided a common answer: the answer lay in the actions of the K–12 school district, particularly with regard to where students were being sent to college. Some community colleges, it seems, achieve racial or economic integration because a disproportionate number of minority or low-income high school graduates are encouraged to attend four-year institutions rather than community colleges. This is consistent with efforts in some districts to ensure that students suited for four-year colleges attend them; particularly those who will most benefit from four-year college attendance. This re-sorting engenders greater balance, and seems to be more common in communities with more resources and strong college preparatory planning in the high schools. Such scenarios can lead to the patterns described earlier, where for example more integrated community colleges have more full-time students on academic tracks (a higher proportion of high school graduates are prepared for full-time work; those at the community college are the place-bound rather than strictly sorted by race or social class). A side effect is that the federal services targeted to economically disadvantaged students are less likely to be found, reducing the number of available staff at the institution (consistent with findings presented earlier).

CONCLUDING THOUGHTS

The primary contribution of this paper is to draw attention to the student composition of community colleges in ways that are cognizant of the important discussions occurring in K–12 education over the past fifty years. It makes little sense to assess the quality of learning environments in such very different ways up and down the educational pipeline. If an economically and racially integrated learning environment is helpful for promoting student achievement, it needs to become a stronger focus and concern in postsecondary education. Of course it is central to discussion of affirmative action policies as they relate to selective, elite institutions, and there have been court cases in several states regarding the support of historically black colleges and universities—but these are conversations affecting a small subset of college students. The vast majority of students attend non-selective institutions, such as community colleges, where the level of "diversity" equates with segregation—not integration.

Admittedly, we raise more challenges and problems than solutions in this paper, partly because of the lack of information with which to do more. This is an area in need of significantly more theorizing and conceptual work, as well as empirical analysis. We need to consider the multiple ways to assess and define isolation in postsecondary education and operationalize the tipping points at which the benefits of integrated environments are achieved. And, while we have provided some starting hypotheses derived from qualitative research, more ideas about how integration could be effectively achieved are needed.

For example, we hypothesize that while the institutions we interviewed did not mention this, integration could be achieved by reducing the difference in costs of attendance between community colleges and four-year institutions. This should reduce the degree to which economically disadvantaged students and those who are loan averse (disproportionately Latinos) are constrained to community colleges and feel freer to choose four-year institutions.

The open door philosophy embraced by community colleges serves a crucial function—ensuring that the colleges reflect their communities. But it also brings challenges; the key one being that the problems of those communities resulting from neighborhood segregation and the concentration of poverty are simply transferred up the educational pipeline. Segregated community colleges not only receive fewer monetary resources, but they likely produce less student learning. That is a problem in need of a worthy solution.

NOTES

1. James S. Coleman et al., *Equality of Educational Opportunity* (Washington, D.C.: U.S. Government Printing Office, 1966), 325.

2. Eric A. Hanushek, John F. Kain, and Steven G. Rivkin, "New Evidence of *Brown v. Board of Education:* The Complex Effects of School Racial Composition on Achievement," NBER Working Paper #8741, National Bureau of Economic Research, 2002. Amy Stuart Wells, Jennifer Jellison Holme, Anita Tijerina Revilla, and Awo Korantemaa Atanda, *Both Sides Now: The Story of School Desegregation's Graduates* (Berkeley: University of California Press, 2008).

3. For a flavor of the debate over the mechanisms undergirding the positive impacts of integration on student outcomes across the K–16 spectrum, see the following examples of recent work in the area: Sara Baker, Adalbert Mayer, and Steven L. Puller, "Do More Diverse Environments Increase the Diversity of Subsequent Interaction? Evidence from Random Dorm Assignment," *Economics Letters* 110, no. 2 (2011): 110–12. Johanne Boisjoly, Greg J. Duncan, Michael Kremer, Dan M. Levy, and Jacque Eccles, "Empathy or Antipathy? The Impact of Diversity," *American Economic Review* 96, no. 5 (2006): 1890–1905. Braz Camargo,

Ralph Stinebrickner, and Todd Stinebrickner, "Interracial Friendships in College," *Journal of Labor Economics* 28, no. 4 (2010): 861–92. Peter Hinrichs, "The Effects of Attending a Diverse College," *Economics of Education Review* 30, no. 2 (2010): 332–41.

4. Amy Stuart Wells, Jacquelyn Duran, and Terrenda White, "Refusing to Leave Desegregation Behind: From Graduates of Racially Diverse Schools to the Supreme Court," *Teachers College Record*, 2008. Amy Stuart Wells and Erica Frankenberg, "The Public Schools and the Challenge of the Supreme Court's Integration Decision," *Phi Delta Kappan* 89, no. 3 (2007): 178–88).

5. Paul Attewell and David E. Lavin, "The Other 75%: College Education Beyond the Elite," Weinberg Seminar Remarks, April 15, 2008. Data are from the Beginning Postsecondary Students Longitudinal Study.

6. We acknowledge that the open door applies only to the very initial point of enrollment. Placement testing means that students are sorted and denied access to a variety of programs almost immediately after that point, and fiscal constraints leading to full classes often diminish the value of the open door entirely.

7. There are exceptions. For example, the NAACP is currently pursuing a lawsuit in Georgia charging that the state has a "dual system of higher education" and has failed to desegregate its historically black and white colleges and universities. *Georgia State Conference of NAACP Branches et al. v. State of Georgia et al.*, Georgia Middle District Court, Case 1:2010cv00041, http://www.courthousenews.com/2010/04/07/NAACP.pdf

8. We acknowledge that this is a big "if." The literature on the effects of integration on schooling outcomes has not grappled sufficiently with selection bias and also has not accounted for the seemingly positive results of fully or nearly segregated schooling, such as that occurring in historically black colleges and universities (HCBUs). By drawing attention to the levels of segregation in community colleges we do not intend in this paper to suggest a new normative focus that would cast HBCU or Hispanic serving institutions or tribal colleges as problematic. First, we note that many of these institutions are in fact substantially integrated by race/ethnicity, but also more importantly that they are segregated by virtue of explicit mission and origins—not defacto by neighborhood composition. The effects are therefore likely different as well.

9. "News from Educational Leadership and Policy Analysis: Clif Conrad's Truth-Telling and Testifying," *Learning Connections*, Spring-Summer 2012, http://news.education.wisc.edu/news-publications/newsletter/archive/2012-spring-summer/clif-conrad-testifying.

10. Economists, for example, have written some of the very small number of empirical studies of segregation in higher education and focus exclusively on four-year institutions. See Charles T. Clotfelter, *After Brown: The Rise and Retreat of School Desegregation* (Princeton N.J.: Princeton University Press, 2004). Also Peter Hinrichs, "An Empirical Analysis of Racial Segregation in Higher Education," paper presented at the Association for Public Policy Analysis and Management Fall

Conference November 8-10, 2012, Baltimore, Maryland, http://www9.georgetown.
edu/faculty/plh24/Hinrichs_segregation_092012.pdf.

11. Sara Goldrick-Rab,"Challenges and Opportunities for Improving Community College Student Outcomes," *Review of Educational Research* 80, no. 3 (2010):
437–69.

12. See endnote 2.

13. The same issue exists in K–12 education. See Roslyn Arlin Mickelson, "The
Reciprocal Relationship between Housing and School Integration," National Coali-
tion on School Diversity, September 2011, http://www.school-diversity.org/pdf/
DiversityResearchBriefNo7.pdf.

14. For example, see "Projects: The College Match Program: Overview," MDRC,
http://www.mdrc.org/project/college-match-program#featured_content.

15. More information on IPEDS is available at the National Center for Education
Statistics website, http://nces.ed.gov/ipeds & www.aspenccprize.org. All geographic
measures come from the 2010 American Community Survey five-year estimates.
More information is available at the U.S. Census FactFinder website, http://fact
finder2.census.gov. With regard to the Aspen Prize, during 2010–11, Aspen solicited
an array of information from community colleges applying for its $1 million prize.
Specifically, 120 institutions were selected to compete and provide information
through a lengthy questionnaire in which they described a "specific range of student
success data as well as [provided] narratives from college leaders describing concrete
examples of practices that have led to excellent student outcomes." Since all of the
institutions involved consented to the use of that information for research purposes,
data for this study included both IPEDS institutional measures for nearly all community colleges nationally, coupled with detailed questionnaire data from the Aspen
sample. Institutions invited to compete for the Aspen Prize were explicitly selected
based on IPEDS information regarding "institutional performance, improvement,
and equity on student retention and completion measures" (round 2 application
instructions). Thus, the competition targeted institutions displaying recent improvements in the success of racial minority and low-income students, though a range
remains among these in terms of their overall levels of diversity.

16. We primarily used geographic predictors and not organizational predictors
because these are arguably endogenous to the outcome of interest—the degree of
diversity. For example, colleges may choose to offer more transfer or degree programs in response to their student population, rather than attracting specific students because of those programs.

17. Participation in the Aspen competition is nonrandom and the ninety-nine
institutions in the subsample differ from the national sample in several ways. We
nonetheless use the data as best we can to gain insights into college activities.
We code the qualitative survey data using the software package Dedoose utilizing responses to the following questions posted by Aspen to participating colleges:
(1) *Institutional Mission: In approximately 100 words, describe your mission, the*

populations you serve, and the programs you offer. Here, we are primarily interested in how the college characterized the racial or ethnic composition of the population served, and whether the mission included an explicit mention of diversity. (2) *External Partners: On no more than one page total, please list external entities (including individual and consortia from K–12, business, non-profit, research, four-year colleges or other sectors) with which your community college is engaged in partnerships that are important to the student outcomes your institution has achieved. Provide a brief explanation (no more than 50 words for each) of the role these partnerships have played at your institution.* We code responses for any indication that partnerships are explicitly undertaken to either in response to diversity or to create diversity. (3) *In 500 or fewer words, summarize the specific programs or factors that you believe have contributed to success in student completion, improvements over time in student completion, or specific achievements demonstrated in your completion data.* We code responses for how success is defined (including any mentions of diversity), as well as programs explicitly undertaken to either in response to diversity or to create diversity. (5) *In one page or less, please provide a statement explaining why your community college has achieved excellent student outcomes, is positioned to continue improving such outcomes in the future, and should win the Aspen Prize for Community College Excellence.* We code responses for how success is defined and any discussion of specific diversity policies and practices in these closing statements.

18. The IPEDS includes two very different institutional measures of Pell receipt. The first represents percent Pell receipt among all students at the institution, while the second is limited to full-time, first-time, degree-seeking students. Although the latter measure only includes a fraction of students who attend community colleges, the proportion of Pell recipients among this group is significantly larger than among all undergraduates. We know that each year part-time students, older students and independent students are far less likely to complete the FAFSA than more "traditional" students even though many would be eligible to receive the grant (Mark Kantrowitz, "Analysis of Why Some Students Do Not Apply for Financial Aid," April 27, 2009, http://wwww.finaid.org/educators/20090427CharacteristicsOfNon Applicants.pdf). We therefore decided to use the full-time, first-time, degree-seeking measure as the more conservative and realistic representation of low-income enrollment at an institution.

19. We defined minority students as those who are neither non-Hispanic white nor Asian. When calculating institutional percentages of racial/ethnic minority enrollment we removed all students categorized as "race/ethnicity unknown" from the total enrollment number before using it as our denominator. This "unknown" category ranged from 0 to 9,833 students per institution, but had a median value of 167. We made the decision to remove these students from our race/ethnicity calculations rather than make assumptions regarding their race/ethnicity which would have been little more than guesswork on our part.

20. We use the term racial/ethnic minority in the sense that African American, Latino, Asian, and Native American students still comprise a numerical minority of the total school population, and white students are still numerically a majority of the student enrollment.

21. We were initially suspicious that findings showing large differences across groups may have been heavily influenced by the 112 California colleges in our sample—fully 12 percent of the total. We therefore ran a second round of comparisons excluding these colleges but found no differences in the pattern of comparisons, only in the individual point estimates.

22. In the 2010 IPEDS, reporting of staff race was voluntary and only 39 percent of the colleges in our sample actually did so. Because reporting was likely nonrandom within the sample, caution should be exercised in the generalizability of the observed group comparisons.

The Role of Race, Income, and Funding on Student Success:
An Institutional Level Analysis of California Community Colleges

TATIANA MELGUIZO and HOLLY KOSIEWICZ

The United States is no longer considered the world leader in producing the largest proportion of young adults with college degrees. Out of the twenty-five countries belonging to the Organization for Economic Co-operation and Development (OECD), the United States moved from being ranked first in 1995 to fourteenth in 2008 in the percent of students who entered college and obtained a four-year degree.[1] Even more troubling is the stubbornly wide gap in four-year degree attainment rates between students of different socioeconomic, racial, and ethnic backgrounds. Recent statistics show that 26 percent of low-income students attain a bachelor's degree, compared with 59 percent of high-income students within six years.[2] Similarly, 41 percent of white students who started at four-year institution in 2004 graduated with a bachelor's

We would like to thank Rick Kahlenberg at The Century Foundation for inviting us to contribute to this volume and for his thoughtful feedback throughout the process. Special thanks to Josh Wyner from The Aspen Institute for sharing a dataset describing the institutional characteristics of the community colleges in the country. We also want to thank Colleen Moore, Nancy Shulock, and Keith Witham for insightful comments and suggestions on earlier drafts. Finally, we want to note the invaluable research assistance that Angela Yan provided in helping us create the final dataset for the project.

degree, compared with 28 percent of Latino students and 20 percent of African-American students.[3]

In 2009, the Obama administration attempted to address these issues in part through the American Graduation Initiative, which would have invested approximately $12 billion in community colleges over ten years to help students progress through college to a certificate or a degree. Even though the initiative was rejected by the Senate, partly due to contracted budgets, it strongly communicated that community colleges ought to play an increasingly larger role in producing college degrees (that is, associate degrees, and baccalaureate degree attainment rates through transfer) and preparing low-income and racial/ethnic minorities for the workforce (that is, certificates related to local market demands). To harness this potential, community colleges will need to increase over-all student success, especially for high needs students, in an environment where state and local funding is decreasing. Recent figures estimated by Anthony P. Carnevale and Jeff Strohl of Georgetown University illustrate that the proportion of low-income and racial and ethnic minorities first enrolling at a community college has been increasing over time.[4] And according to recent findings from the Delta Cost Project at the American Institutes for Research, public community colleges receive substantially less state dollars per full time equivalent student than public four-year colleges.[5] Since significant proportions of low-income and minority students attend public two-year institutions, community colleges have enormous potential to narrow the racial and ethnic achievement gap that has historically plagued higher education.

In this paper, we explore the relationships between a community col-lege's effectiveness and three factors: the amount of state and local fund-ing it receives, the racial and ethnic composition of its student body, and its socioeconomic status measured by median income levels of house-holds surrounding the college. We draw on four strands of research to frame our analysis: (1) human capital theory,[6] (2) school finance,[7] (3) school-based poverty,[8] and (4) school segregation.[9] To measure com-munity college effectiveness, we employ California's Student Progress and Achievement Rate (SPAR).[10] We use this indicator instead of other performance measures because it is calculated based on a student cohort model and measures multiple outcomes for community college students.

The study employs a unique dataset constructed using recently released state and national data from the California Community College Chancellor's Office (CCCCO), the State of California, and the National Center of Education Statistics (NCES). Although the study's findings are calculated using data on California community colleges, they provide important insights for other community colleges across the nation as they struggle with decreasing public financial support, maintaining their mission of open access, and providing high quality education, particularly for the most underserved student groups.

This study presents descriptive statistics and results from bivariate and regression analyses to better understand the associations between these three factors and SPAR. It is important to note that the results presented in this paper are correlational, not causal. Indeed, it is likely that different types of colleges attract different types of students. For example, community colleges located in more affluent areas may be better at attracting academically average or above average students as well as students who are highly motivated to perform well in college. Thus differences on any measure of student success, including SPAR, may be explained more by the types of students community colleges attract than by their ability to better prepare their students. This is known as self-selection in economic literature. Given that we are unable to control for self-selection in our analysis, our estimates may be biased. Future papers examining the relationship between student success and racial and ethnic diversity as well as neighborhood wealth should control for this bias before making any type of causal inference.

The material in this paper is presented in four stages. First, we provide a brief description of California's community colleges, paying attention in particular to how they are governed and funded by state government. Second, we present a description of the sample, variables, and methods used to conduct our analysis. Third, we report the results of the analyses. Fourth, we offer some initial conclusions and policy directions in this area.

A DEMOGRAPHIC PROFILE OF
CALIFORNIA COMMUNITY COLLEGE STUDENTS

California has the largest community college system in the nation. It is composed of 112 community colleges and 72 districts. According to the Legislative Analyst Office, the State of California enrolls about 22 percent of all U.S. community college students. Recent estimates based on 2008 data show that about 1.6 million full-time equivalent (FTE) students attend a California community college. Over 50 percent of these students are categorized as underrepresented minorities (that is, Latino, African American, and Native American students).[11] Compared to the past, California community colleges are enrolling more Latino students and fewer white students.[12] From 1997 to 2003, the percentage of Latino community college students grew by five points; conversely, the percentage of white students dropped by six points during the same time period.[13] These shifts reflect parallel demographic changes in the general U.S. population.

One reason why many students, particularly underrepresented students, start their higher education at a community college in California is that they are open access, have among the lowest student fees in the country, and allow needy students to qualify for fee waivers. Such provisions make attending college a possibility for many students who may not have the financial means or adequate preparation to attend a four-year institution at the start of their college experience.

FUNDING STRUCTURE OF THE CALIFORNIA COMMUNITY COLLEGE SYSTEM

The current funding structure of the California Community College System (CCCS) is built out of two major regulations: Proposition 13 (passed in 1978) and Proposition 98 (passed in 1988). Proposition 13 limits the amount of tax that can be levied on property, effectively transferring the responsibility of funding community colleges from the local to the state government. Proposition 98 requires a minimum percentage of state revenues to be spent on the K–14 system. After its passage, Proposition 98 guaranteed California community colleges 10.9 percent of the state's education funding, but the system traditionally has received a slightly lower percentage and this has been a point of contention with the K–12 system. Because of this joint funding structure, community colleges share 34 percent of the K–14 state budget with primary and secondary schools. Consequently, community colleges often receive less funding than what was initially set aside for them. This translates into billions of dollars in lost revenue for California's community colleges.

Each fiscal year, the state allocates operating funds to the community college system, which are then reallocated to the 72 community college districts. Before 2006, the state used program-based funding (PBF), which is a textbook example of an incremental budget formula that uses the previous year to adjust for inflation, expansion of services, as well as differences in local property taxes from 1992 until 2006. The formula was established in the early 1990s, and it served to allocate resources until it was changed after the passage of SB 361 in 2007. The goal of

SB 361 was to equalize funding and strived for fairness, simplicity and predictability. It equalized funding for credit, non-credit, and enhanced non-credit FTE students across all districts, took into account economies of scales, and tried to ensure that smaller districts received adequate funds to operate and encourage student success. A limitation of the current funding structure is that it fails to factor in the increasing numbers of students from academically and culturally diverse backgrounds that California community colleges seek to serve. Consequently, the amount of funding community colleges receive is based primarily on the number of students they enroll the previous year and not on the *type of student* they enroll. In addition to these inequities, there is evidence that the amount of funding community colleges receive is not adequate to provide the quality of services needed to promote student success. There is also evidence showing that California has one of the highest student-to-counselor ratios in the nation, with ratios reaching 1,700 to 1.[14] Finally, even though the state has established a target funding level for its community colleges, it has funded the system well below this percentage for decades. Because of this, many community colleges in California lack the resources and funding to develop or expand new programs and improve the quality of current services.

GOVERNANCE FRAMEWORK OF
CALIFORNIA COMMUNITY COLLEGES

The framework that governs community colleges is similar to that which governs K–12. Although community colleges were legally separated from the K–12 system in 1967, community colleges are still governed at the local level. Each community college district is an independent local government entity overseen by an elected board of trustees. Local boards are in charge of developing administrative policies, developing the curriculum, selecting program offerings, and negotiating with unions representing instructional staff.[15] These boards appoint a district chancellor or a college president to serve as the chief executive officer. Like the K–12 system in the state, California community colleges are heavily unionized. Collective bargaining units represent most of the employees at community colleges, who have tenure and benefits similar to K–12 teachers. Support staff are hired and promoted under a civil service system. The heavily decentralized governance structure of community colleges stand in contrast with the more centralized governing structure of the University of California (UC) and California State

University (CSU) systems. The UC and CSU systems each have a unique governing board that provides system-wide administrative and curricular guidelines, while guaranteeing individual campus autonomy.

METHODOLOGY

Data

To conduct this study, we draw data from four state sources and one national source: (1) the Accountability Report for California Community Colleges (ARCC), (2) the Management and Information System (MIS), (3) the Fiscal Data Abstract, (4) California Postsecondary Education Commission (CPEC), and the (5) Integrated Postsecondary Education Data System (IPEDS).[16]

Sample

The final sample is composed of 107 of the 112 community colleges that make up the California Community College System. This sample represents approximately 95 percent of the colleges in the system.[17] Our data for different variables stem from 2000 to 2012, but in most cases we are able to employ several years of data to smooth out any year-to-year variations.

Dependent Variables

The main dependent variable that we use in our analysis is SPAR, which is measured annually as part of the ARCC. The ARCC is published by the California Community College Chancellor's Office (CCCCO) in order to meet a legislative requirement stated in Assembly Bill 1417. The ARCC presents a series of performance indicators that assess community colleges on their multiple missions. We also examine the percent of students who transferred to a four-year institution, the total number of associate degrees awarded, and the total number of certificates awarded in our bivariate analysis.

Student Progress and Achievement Rate (SPAR). The Student Progress and Achievement Rate is considered by ARCC as a community college's overall measure of success. It is calculated based on tracking the progress and outcomes of entering student cohorts over six years. First-time students who show intent to complete (that is, who over six years completed at least twelve credits and attempted degree-applicable math or English course or a threshold-level occupational course) and who achieve any of the following outcomes within six years: (1) transferred to a four-year college, (2) attained an associate in arts degree or an associate in science degree, (3) earned a certificate (18 units or more, or 12–17 units if the certificate was approved by the chancellor's office) or (4) achieved "transfer directed" or "transfer prepared" status increase a community college's SPAR rate. To facilitate our analysis, we averaged SPAR over three cohorts of students: 2003–04 to 2005–06. The average SPAR rate over these three cohorts is 52.2 percent; SPAR rates range from 26.9 to 70.7 percent.

Percent of Transfer Students. Percent of transfer students is a cohort-based variable that colleges calculate by tracking cohorts of first-time students for six years to determine if the students show a behavioral intent to transfer. In other words, if a student has completed 12 credit units and attempted transfer-level math or English, he or she is considered on a track toward transfer. We averaged percent of transfer students across six cohorts of students (2000–01 to 2005–06); the average percent of students who transferred in our dataset is 38.9 across all community colleges; transfer rates range from 13.3 to 59.5 percent across the cohorts we examine.

Total Number of Associate Degrees. Total number of associate degrees is measured as the total number of associate degrees awarded in a specific academic year. We calculated an average for total number of degrees awarded across six academic years: 2005–06 to 2010–11. Over these years, California community colleges awarded a total of 84,633 associate degrees. The number of associate degrees awarded ranged from 107 to 2,663.

Total Number of Certificates. Total number of certificates is measured as the total number of certificates awarded—irrespective of the credits required—in a specific academic year. We calculated an average for the total number of certificates awarded across six academic years: 2005–06 to 2010–11. The number of certificates totaled 33,193 and ranged from 23 to 1,859 certificates.

Independent Variables

Proportion of Underrepresented Minorities. In California, underrepresented minorities are students who consider themselves African-American, Latino and Native-American. For this study, we used a six-year average (2005–06 to 2010–11) of the proportion of students enrolled in a college that was African-American or Latino as a proxy for the racial and ethnic composition of the college student body. The proportion of underrepresented minorities across sampled colleges ranged from 11.8 to 90.9 percent.

College Socioeconomic Status. We measure a college's socioeconomic status by the median family income of the location[18] surrounding each community college as measured in 2012. Median family income of location ranged from \$29,221 to \$157,995.[19] Even though this variable is correlated with local funding (r = 0.31), it cannot fully explain the amount of funding community colleges received through local property taxes. We thus argue that college socioeconomic status cannot be considered a strong proxy for local funding.

State and Local Funding. We measure state and local funding by the amount of funding that a community college received from state and local government per FTE in 2010. The average amount of state funding granted per California community college student was approximately \$3,370; the average amount of local funding granted per California community college student was roughly \$2,290. State funding ranged from \$587 to \$6,583 per FTE; local funding ranged from \$758 to \$7,870 per FTE.

Model

The equation below specifies the main model:

$$\text{SPAR}_c = \alpha_c + \text{URMQ}_c\beta_{\text{URMQ}} + \text{SESCOLLQ}_c\beta_{\text{SESCOLLQ}} + \text{SFUND}_c\beta_{\text{SFUND}} + \text{LFUND}_c\beta_{\text{LFUND}} + \text{CONTROLS}_c\beta_{\text{CONTROLS}} + u_c$$

where URMQ is the percent of underrepresented minority students enrolled in a college, divided into quartiles; SESCOLLQ is the college socioeconomic status divided into quartiles; SFUND is the amount of state funding a college receives per FTE in thousands; LFUND is the amount of local funding a college receives per FTE in thousands; and CONTROLS is a vector of variables that measure other student population and institutional characteristics. We use a stepwise regression approach to run several models that measure the relationship between a college's overall student success and its racial and ethnic student makeup, socioeconomic status, and the amount of state and local funding it received.

According to University of Chicago professor Gary S. Becker,[20] these models can be considered simple production functions and ought to control for variables that, according to economic and education literature, are associated with degree and certificate attainment.

Aggregated at the collegiate-level, control variables include a number of student demographic characteristics: female (six-year average), traditional age (six-year average base category nontraditional age over 25 years old), and part-time (six year average of proportion of students attending part-time). We also control for the academic preparation of the types of students a college enrolls in two ways. First, we factor in the average Academic Performance Index (API) score for high schools that feed into each community college from 2005 to 2010. Second, we include a variable that measures the number of students who were placed into the third and fourth lowest levels of the developmental math sequence at their community college[21] between 2004 and 2006. We include additional controls for institutional characteristics from IPEDS such as: institutional size (large versus small), vocational quartile (quartile based on the proportion of vocational certificates awarded), and location (base category urban).

RESULTS

Bivariate Analysis

Association between Proportion of URM and Measures of Student Success. Consistent with findings from the K–12 literature,[22] we found statistically significant differences in the proportion of URM students enrolled in a college and a college's SPAR rate. Whereas colleges in the lowest URM student quartile (11.8 percent 21.5 percent) exhibited an average SPAR rate of 57 percent, colleges in the highest URM student quartile (48.7 percent to 90.9 percent) showed a SPAR rate of less than 45 percent, a difference of approximately twelve percentage points (see Table 1). We found a similar statistical difference when examining the relationship between the proportion of URM students and percent of students exhibiting a behavioral intent to transfer. Colleges in the lowest URM student quartile showed an average transfer rate of 42 percent compared with a transfer rate of 33 percent for colleges in the highest URM student quartile. However, we found no statistically significant differences of attending colleges with higher proportions of URM in terms of students obtaining an associate degree or certificate. These contradictory findings may stem from the way these performance variables are measured.

Association between Socioeconomic Status and Measures of Student Success. Results from our correlational analysis also suggest that college socioeconomic status is positively and statistically associated with SPAR and percent of transfer students, but bear no statistically significant relationship with associate degrees or certificates (see Table 1). The fact that transfer and SPAR are cohort-based measures suggest again that it is important to examine outcomes for cohorts of students instead of the total number of awards conferred in a specific academic year, which may include students from many different cohorts.

Association between State and Local Funding and Measures of Student Success. We find a negative and statistically significant association between state funding and SPAR and percent of transfer students; conversely, we find a positive and statistically significant association between local funding and SPAR and percent of transfer students (see Table 2). With respect to the average number of degrees granted (that is, associate degrees and certificates), we find that they are not statistically related with state or local funding.

We also find that the amount of state funding a community college receives per FTE does not statistically differ by the proportion of URM students they enroll (see Table 3). For example, colleges with student populations composed of less than approximately 22 percent of underrepresented students (lowest quartile) received on average $3,101 per FTE while colleges with student populations composed of more than 49 percent of underrepresented students (highest quartile) received almost $3,650 per FTE. The fact that colleges irrespective of the proportion of URM students they enroll receive roughly the same of amount of state funding per FTE may be traceable to the current funding formula. Our results also suggest that colleges with student populations composed of higher proportions of URM students receive less local funding compared with colleges with students populations composed of lower proportions of URM students. These differences are statistically significant

TABLE 1
Average Educational Outcomes by Racial and Ethnic Composition of Students and College Socioeconomic Status

	State Average	Proportion of Under-represented Minorities				Local Median Family Income (College SES)			
		Lowest	Mid-Low	Mid-High	Highest	Lowest	Mid-Low	Mid-High	Highest
Student Progress and Achievement Rate (SPAR): degree/certificate/transfer—three cohorts	52%	57%	55%	51%	45% *	45%	53%	53%	57% *
Transfer—six cohorts	39%	42%	42%	38%	33% **	32%	38%	39%	47% **
Associate degrees (AA)—six year average	749	657	850	795	717	612	860	877	705
Certificates—six year average	373	262	383	392	492	260	433	509	336

* p < 0.05
** p < 0.01

Note: According to the College Board, 84,374 associate degrees and 47,884 certificates were awarded by California community colleges in 2009–10. ARCC reports that 112,327 were awarded by California community colleges in 2010–11.

Source: Data compiled from California Community College Chancellor's Office Management and Information System (MIS) and U.S. Department of Education, Institute of Education Sciences, National Center for Education Statistics, Integrated Postsecondary Education Data System (IPEDS).

TABLE 2
Average Educational Outcomes by Average State and Local Funding per FTE

	State Average	State Funding				Local Funding			
		Lowest	Mid-Low	Mid-High	Highest	Lowest	Mid-Low	Mid-High	Highest
Student Progress and Achievement Rate (SPAR): degree/certificate/transfer—three cohorts	52%	58%	52%	51%	47% *	48%	50%	54%	58% *
Transfer—six cohorts	39%	43%	40%	39%	32% *	35%	37%	40%	44% *
Associate degrees (AA)—six year average	749	769	693	1001	622	789	884	669	718
Certificates—six year average	373	355	379	437	346	425	416	368	286

* p < 0.01
Source: Data compiled from California Community College Chancellor's Office Management and Information System (MIS) and U.S. Department of Education, Institute of Education Sciences, National Center for Education Statistics, Integrated Postsecondary Education Data System (IPEDS).

TABLE 3
Differences in State and Local Funding per FTE by Racial and Ethnic Distribution of the Students and College Socioeconomic Status

	State		Local	
URM-quartile				
Lowest (11.8%–21.5%)	$3,101		$3,051	*
Mid-low (21.7%–34.8%)	$3,060		$2,431	*
Mid-high (35.2%–48.5%)	$3,669		$1,820	*
Highest (48.7%–90.9%)	$3,649		$1,824	*
SES College-quartile				
Lowest ($29,221–$50,784)	$4,212	*	$1,721	*
Mid-low ($50,932–$62,473)	$3,213	*	$2,210	*
Mid-high ($62,916–$81,617)	$3,340	*	$2,140	*
Highest ($81,718–$157,995)	$2,617	*	$3,042	*

*p < 0.01
Source: Data compiled from California Community College Chancellor's Office Management and Information System (MIS) and U.S. Department of Education, Institute of Education Sciences, National Center for Education Statistics, Integrated Postsecondary Education Data System (IPEDS).

at the one percent level. What these results suggest is that colleges with higher proportions of URM students are not properly compensated by the state for the lower amounts of funding that they received. By contrast, we find that the amount of state and local funding that community colleges receive differ significantly by their socioeconomic status. Colleges located in wealthier areas receive more local funding but less state funding than colleges located in poorer areas (p < 0.01).

In summary, results from our bivariate analysis illustrate that colleges located in the third and fourth quartiles (largest proportions) of URM students report a SPAR rate that are ten and twelve percentage points lower than colleges located in the first quartile (lowest proportion) in terms of SPAR. We found the opposite trend in terms of socioeconomic status of the colleges. Colleges located in the wealthiest areas (fourth quartile) report a SPAR rate that is twelve percentage points higher than colleges located in the poorest areas (first quartile). In the next section, we report results from our regression analysis where we control institutional level and student population factors associated with SPAR.

Regression Analysis

Results from our regression analysis suggest a negative and statistically significant association between the racial and ethnic composition of a college and SPAR. Holding all else constant, we find that colleges where URM students represent between 35 percent and 49 percent of their student population (third quartile) experience about a 5 percent decrease on SPAR compared to colleges where URM students represent less than 22 percent of the student population (first quartile; see Table 4). We see that this statistically significant and negative association prevails and becomes even stronger when we contrast colleges in the highest URM student quartile against those with the lowest quartile of underrepresented minorities on their students' academic performance. Compared with colleges classified as having the lowest proportion of underrepresented students, colleges classified as having the highest proportion of URM (above 49 percent) experience a 10 percent decrease on SPAR holding all else constant. Consistent with economic literature, we observe a negative and statistically significant association between college socioeconomic status and SPAR. Using the highest socioeconomic status quartile as our base category (income > $81,718), colleges located in the lowest income areas (income < $50,784) experience an eight percent decrease on SPAR. Further, colleges located in middle-to-low income areas ($50,784 to $62,473) suffer a loss of over 3 percent on SPAR compared against colleges located in high-income areas.

The above mentioned results suggest that colleges with student populations composed of over 35 percent of underrepresented minorities have significantly lower SPAR rates than less racially isolated colleges. Analogous evidence is found in literature exploring the effects of segregation on student performance at the K–12 level.[23] Similarly, colleges located in less wealthy areas underperform on SPAR compared to those in the highest income areas.

CONCLUSIONS AND IMPLICATIONS FOR FUTURE RESEARCH

Increasing student success in community colleges has become a central policy focus largely tied with maintaining U.S. standing in the global economy. Decreasing government funding and shifts in the demographic profile of community college students have called into question whether higher education systems as currently designed are equipped to increase

TABLE 4
Association between Funding and Student Composition and Student Progress and Attainment Rate (SPAR)

	Model 1	Model 2	Model 3
Underrepresented Minorities *(base lowest quartile)*			
Mid-low (21.7%–48.5%)	−1.81	−1.80	−2.68
	(1.48)	(1.57)	(1.50)
Mid-high (35.2%–48.5%)	−4.00***	−3.742**	−4.50**
	(1.55)	(1.71)	(1.82)
Highest (48.7%–90.9%)	−9.22***	−8.38***	−9.58***
	(1.60)	(1.79)	(2.07)
Socioeconomic Status of Colleges *(base highest quartile)*			
Lowest (< $50,784)	−5.73**	−6.69**	−7.88**
	(1.67)	(1.69)	(1.73)
Mid-low ($50,784–$62,916)	−2.10	−2.72	−3.59*
	(1.51)	(1.51)	(1.44)
Mid-high ($62,916–$81,718)	−1.21	−1.93	−2.68
	(1.46)	(1.51)	(1.46)
Funding			
State	−2.76**	−2.85**	−2.61*
	(0.84)	(1.12)	(1.06)
Local	−0.70	−0.94	−0.72
	(0.73)	(0.81)	(0.76)
Controls			
Student population characteristics	No	No	Yes
Institutional characteristics	No	Yes	Yes
Total	107	107	107

$* p < 0.10$, $** p < 0.05$, $*** p < 0.01$

Note: Demographic controls include: percent of students receiving Board of Governor's fee waivers, percent female, percent part-time, number of students placed into the lowest levels of remedial math, API scores for feeder high schools. Institutional controls include: location of community college, college size, percent of students in a vocational track.

Source: Data compiled from California Community College Chancellor's Office Management and Information System (MIS) and U.S. Department of Education, Institute of Education Sciences, National Center for Education Statistics, Integrated Postsecondary Education Data System (IPEDS).

success for all types of students. This study informs this current discussion by conducting an institutional-level analysis of California community colleges, examining how state and local funding, student racial and ethnic composition, and college socioeconomic status relate with a college's overall student success.

The findings presented in this paper provide evidence showing that colleges serving larger proportions of underrepresented minority students experience on average worse outcomes on various measures of student success compared with colleges with lower proportions of underrepresented minority students. Specifically, we find that colleges with populations composed of over 35 percent of underrepresented minority students experience significantly lower SPAR rates than colleges with less than 22 percent of underrepresented minorities. While this result is to be expected given that African-American and Latino students on average report lower indices of academic achievement during high school and college, the finding holds true even after we control for two institutional level measures of academic preparation: average Academic Performance Index of feeder high schools, and the number of students in the lowest levels of developmental math. The result suggests there may be harms associated with racial and economic isolation at the community college level, mirroring those found at the elementary and secondary levels.

The findings also suggests that California's higher education system has been unsuccessful in remedying systemic and institutional shortcomings to better respond to the academic and nonacademic needs of colleges serving principally underrepresented minorities. As shown in our bivariate results, the amount of state funding that a community college receives is independent of the percent of underrepresented minority students it enrolls. Although the amount of state aid a community college receives depends on a number of factors, the current funding formula for community colleges does not factor in the types of students (that is, ethnicity or socioeconomic status) a community college enrolls.

In light of our findings, we offer two suggestions that policymakers should consider in order to create meaningful and positive change in colleges serving predominately underrepresented minorities.

Address Socioeconomic and Racial Isolation

First, policymakers should consider ways to remedy the impact of socioeconomic and racial isolation at American community colleges. Creative thinking should address ways to create a more optimal economic and racial/ethnic mix at both community colleges and four-year colleges. For example, in California, the UC and CSU systems recently increased the quota of out of state and international students enrolled in their colleges. While such action increases revenue for these two systems, it limits the number of spots available to community college transfer students at public four-year institutions. This could have the effect of making community colleges even more racially and economically isolated, as white and middle-class students may avoid two-year institutions because they may have difficulty transferring to a four-year institution. Efforts should be made instead to make community colleges more attractive to a broad cross-section of students, while opening access at four-year colleges to more economically disadvantaged and minority students. Ensuring that community colleges have more voice in discussions about admissions decisions at four-year colleges may also serve to increase success among community college students.

Rethink Current Funding Mechanisms

State and local funding formulas across the country should recognize that more needs to be done to compensate colleges with larger proportions of underrepresented minority and low-income students. To close this gap, the current funding model should consider allocating additional state funding to community colleges serving these types of students, tying such funding with efforts to improve teaching practices and student services. This type of provision would mimic Title I funding in K–12 schools, which serves to improve performance for schools that serve high-need students.[24] Currently, colleges serving over 25 percent of Latino students are classified as Hispanic Serving Institutions (HSIs) and qualify for receiving additional funding. This policy should be continued and ought to incorporate a performance based measure that provides a premium for HSIs as well as other minority student serving institutions that are effective in increasing success and progress rates for underrepresented minorities.

NOTES

1. *Education at a Glance 2010* (Paris: Organization for Economic Co-operation and Development, 2010).

2. Paul Skomsvold, Alexandria Walton Radford, and Lutz Berkner, "Six-Year Attainment, Persistence, Transfer, Retention, and Withdrawal Rates of Students Who Began PostsecondaryEducation in 2003–04," (NCES 2011-152), U.S. Department

of Education, Institute of Education Sciences, National Center for Educational Statistics, 2011.

3. Thomas D. Snyder and Sally A. Dillow, *Digest of Education Statistics 2011* (Washington, D.C.: U.S. Department of Education, National Center for Education Statistics, 2012).

4. Anthony P. Carnevale and Jeff Strohl, "How Increasing College Access Is Increasing Inequality and What To Do about It," in *Rewarding Strivers: Helping Low-Income Students Succeed in College,* ed. Richard D. Kahlenberg (New York: The Century Foundation Press, 2010), 71–201.

5. Donna M. Desrochers and Jane V. Wellman, *Trends in College Spending 1999–2009* (Washington, D.C.: Delta Project on Postsecondary Education Costs, Productivity, and Accountability, 2011), http://www.deltacostproject.org/resources/pdf/Trends2011_Final_090711.pdf.

6. Gary S. Becker, *Human Capital: A Theoretical and Empirical Analysis, with Special Reference to Education,* 3d. ed. (Chicago: University of Chicago Press, 1994).

7. Eric A. Hanushek, "Assessing the Effects of School Resources on Student Performance: An Update," *Educational Evaluation and Policy Analysis* 19 (1997): 141–64.

8. John S. Coleman et al., *Equality of Educational Opportunity* (Washington, D.C.: U.S. Government Printing Office, 1966).

9. Gary Orfield, *Schools More Separate: Consequences of a Decade of Resegregation* (Cambridge, Mass.: The Civil Rights Project, Harvard University, 2001).

10. SPAR is calculated using the total number of first-time who showed intent to complete. In order to know what proportion of the full time equivalent (FTE) students were represented in the cohort, we used IPEDS to estimate the ratio of the number of first-time full-time degree seeking students to the total number of FTE students. For the 2005 academic year, the California community college system reported a total of 439,053 Fall FTE students enrolled and of those only 71,502 were first-time full-time certificate-seeking students. This means that the cohort represents about 16 percent of the total number of students enrolled in the community colleges. We used IPEDS to calculate this proportion for the years 2005 to 2008 and our estimate ranged between 16 percent to 23 percent. This might be a lower bound estimate as we are not taking into account part-time students who showed intent to complete.

11. Legislative Analyst Office, "The 2012–13 Budget: Proposition 98 Education Analysis," February 6, 2012, //www.lao.ca.gov/analysis/2012/education/proposition-98-020612.aspx.

12. Public Policy Institute of California, "California's Community College Students," *California Counts: Population Trends and Profiles* 8, no.2 (November 2006), http://www.ppic.org/content/pubs/cacounts/CC_1106RSCC.pdf.

13. Ibid.

14. Gale Holland, "California's Community Colleges Near the Breaking Point," *Los Angeles Times,* February 3, 2009, articles.latimes.com/2009/feb/03/local/me-transfer3.

15. Patrick Murphy, Max Neiman, and Jelena Hasbrouck, "Exploring Candidates, Elections, Campaigns, and Expenditures in California Community College

Districts, 2004–2010," Research and Occasional Paper Series: CSHE11.12, Center for Studies in Higher Education, University of California, Berkeley, October 2012.

16. The ARCC, MIS, and Fiscal Data Abstract are managed by the California Community College Chancellor's Office (CCCCO); IPEDS is published by the U.S. Department of Education, Institute of Education Sciences, National Center for Education Statistics. CPEC was managed by the State of California (recently eliminated). California Postsecondary Education Commission, "Ethnicity Snapshots," http://www.cpec.ca.gov/StudentData/EthSnapshotGraph.asp (retrieved August 28, 2012).

17. Although 112 community colleges make up the California community college system, longitudinal data on four newly instituted colleges were missing. Therefore regression analysis could not be conducted on these colleges.

18. Initially we used the Board of Governors Fee Waiver (BOGFW) as a proxy for the socioeconomic status of colleges. In California, a student who belongs to a family of four with an income of less than $33,525 receives a fee waiver. In our analysis, we found a strong correlation between BOGFW and state funding (78 percent). This strong correlation is explained by the fact that colleges in California receive additional funding if their students qualify for this fee waiver. For this reason we decided against using this variable in our analysis in favor of median family income to determine the socioeconomic status of each college.

19. The variable median family income of location is based on 2012 data and calculated by the Aspen Institute. Data on college socioeconomic status were unavailable for previous years.

20. Becker, *Human Capital*.

21. Although we consider this variable the best proxy for academic preparation of entering students, it does suffer several limitations. First, given that community colleges are open access institutions, they cannot use the SAT or other measures to select students so we are unable to use this variable as a control for academic preparation. Second, the meaningfulness of API feeder high schools is limited given that even though a majority of community college students tend to attend two-year colleges in their neighborhoods, some do attend community colleges that are far away from their homes. Given that we did not have access to student's high school transcripts, we considered these two variables to be the best proxies for a student's academic preparation.

22. "Annotated Bibliography: The Impact of School-Based Poverty Concentration on Academic Achievement and Student Outcomes," Poverty and Race Research Action Council, Washington, D.C., http://www.prrac.org/pdf/annotated_bibliography_on_school_poverty_concentration.pdf.

23. Ibid.

24. The state of California is exploring the use of a weighted formula to allocate resources in K–12 (Legislative Analyst Office, "The 2012–13 Budget: Proposition 98 Education Analysis"). Given the similar governance and funding structure of the CCCS to the K–12 system, it would be important to explore whether this type of funding would also result in reductions in educational attainment gaps between URM and white and Asian and Pacific Islanders in community colleges.

Index

About the Background
Paper Authors

SANDY BAUM is senior fellow at the George Washington University Graduate School of Education and Human Development and professor emerita of economics at Skidmore College. She has written and spoken extensively on issues relating to college access, college pricing, student aid policy, student debt, and college affordability. She has coauthored the College Board's annual publications, *Trends in Student Aid* and *Trends in College Pricing* since 2002. She led a Brookings Institution study group that issued its report, *Beyond Need and Merit: Strengthening State Grant Programs* in 2012. The Rethinking Pell Grants Study Group, which she led under the auspices of the College Board, issued its report in April 2013.

SARA GOLDRICK-RAB is associate professor of educational policy studies and sociology at University of Wisconsin–Madison, senior scholar at the Wisconsin Center for the Advancement of Postsecondary Education, and an affiliate of the Institute for Research on Poverty, the LaFollette School of Public Affairs, and the Wisconsin Center for Educational Research. She was named a 2010 William T. Grant Scholar for her project "Rethinking College Choice in America." She was also a 2004 Rising Scholar in Higher Education by the National Forum on Higher Education for the Public Good and a 2006 National Academy of Education/Spencer Foundation postdoctoral fellow. She is the coauthor of *Putting Poor People to Work: How the Work-First Idea Eroded College Access the Poor* (Russell Sage, 2006), which was a finalist for the C. Wright Mills award.

PETER KINSLEY is a doctoral candidate in educational policy studies at the University of Wisconsin—Madison. His research bridges the fields of postsecondary education policy, sociology, and family studies by focusing on college persistence and attainment among low-income students, as well as the role that family networks play in their postsecondary success. He has regularly presented his work at national education conferences including the American Educational Research Association, the International Sociological Association, and the Commission on Adult Basic Education.

HOLLY KOSIEWICZ is a PhD student in the urban education policy program at the University of Southern California. She uses qualitative and quantitative methods to evaluate policies that seek to improve success among college students who are low-income and of color.

CHARLES KUROSE is an independent consultant to the College Board. His research focuses on student financial aid and institutional finance in higher education. Through the College Board's Advocacy and Policy Center he works on projects such as the *Trends in Student Aid* and *Trends in College Pricing* annual publications. He also has worked on projects about higher education finance organized by the Lumina Foundation, the Brookings Institution, and George Washington University's Graduate School of Education and Human Development. Prior to his current professional activities, he worked at the Spencer Foundation as a research associate.

TATIANA MELGUIZO is an associate professor in the Rossier School of Education, University of Southern California. She works in the field of economics of higher education. She uses quantitative methods of analysis to study the association of different factors such as student trajectories as well as public policies on the persistence and educational outcomes of minority and low-income students. Her work has been published in *Education Evaluation and Policy Analysis, Teachers College Record*, the *Journal of Higher Education*, the *Review of Higher Education, Research in Higher Education*, and *Higher Education*.